Nocturne

111 POEMS BY
GEORG TRAKL

edited & translated from the German
by Daniele Pantano

with a foreword by Joshua Weiner

BLACK LAWRENCE PRESS

Black Lawrence Press

Executive Editor: Diane Goettel
Book Cover Design: Zoe Norvell
Cover Art: "DAME DE TU ALIENTO" by Ángel Pascual Rodrigo
Book Interior Design: Serena Solin

ISBN: 9781625571984

Published 2026 by Black Lawrence Press.
Printed in the United States.

Contents

Traklwelt

A world of light and dark, primary colors (blue, white, green, yellow, red; and also gold and silver) expressionistically saturating objects and phenomena outside the bounds of nature; a place of stillness and violence; the *Naturlyrik* of German Romanticism infected by modern cities of glass and steel; all manner of flora and fauna, of illicit desires (incest), impossible music, windows like eyes opening and closing; deep solitude, contorted melancholy; bodies of water holding secrets; earthly energies laden with evil and with good; phenomenal life innocent of human speech; rich thresholds into sinister evening shadows; deliriums and dreams, heretical psalms, whispers lost in storms; harmonies and torments, damnations and despairs, derangement, decay, rotten flesh, smoking blood, joy in gloom, peace in intimacies with death; shepherds, fishermen, hunters moving through landscapes of lost pastoralism; blurred visions and hallucinatory clarities; wandering monks and castles; black winds and black wings; broken crosses, shattered eyes, hesitant footsteps, grimaces and trumpet blasts; the disappearing voices of angels and lepers, bells in the distance, fragrance of forgotten legends... It's a spooky world, a world in which the dead appear more alive, more present than the living; a world of fragments and remnants of a world disappeared yet still somehow manifest and ebbing out, purgatorial, here and gone, liminal, seductive, full of foreboding, grief, and difficult sublime beauty; a world, finally, that we recognize, in its stark terror and destruction, as fully ours: the world of Trakl, *Traklwelt*—how are we meant to feel about it? How do we enter?

This summer, I'm thinking about our world (which was never not *not* Trakl's) a world at war with over fifty armed conflicts, a world on fire, and a rising global nostalgia before AI tempted us at our fingertips and pushed us to check out of our humanity, before "social media" degraded meaningful sociality; a world of forty-two million refugees (and counting) fleeing violence, persecution, climate catastrophe, and the collapsing physical and psychic environment, the rise of autocratic nationalism and super-hyper-capitalism. In "Year," Trakl writes, "beneath ancient cypress trees / the tears of nightly images gather by the well; / Golden eye of inception, dark patience of the end." Those "nightly images" are drawn today from the abyssal well of digital platforms; "golden eye of inception" indeed. What does the ear see, what does the eye hear? What do we experience in Traklwelt? What's there for us now? For one thing, and most immediate, the senses are alive there: blue deer, ringing gold, sorrowful trees, dark silence, cold sparkle, purple wind, red laughter. Is this madness? It's an instrument of vision rinsed of quotidian conventions; it's not your grandfather's Eden; but it restores, at one limit of what language can do, a primary experience of sensuous life.

The synesthesia, a mixing of the senses, that one finds everywhere in Trakl was one of the stylistic impulses of an early Expressionism (1905), the European art movement he is most associated with. In addition to a host of aspects and characteristics—an emphasis on the image as a medium of direct experience; a suppression of argument, explanation, analysis, and other modes of discursiveness; juxtaposition of fragments without explicit syntactical linking (parataxis and associational logic);

an instilled ambiguity that arises from grammatical suspension, etc...—we could also place Trakl in proximity to others associated with Viennese modernism, such as Karl Kraus, Ludwig Wittgenstein, Adolf and Bessie Loos, Oskar Kokoschka, Arnold Schönberg (all of whom he connected with thanks to Ludwig von Ficker, his editor at the avant-garde journal *Der Brenner*), as well as earlier French Symbolists such as Baudelaire, Rimbaud, and Verlaine, with whom he identified artistically (introduced through childhood reading encouraged by a French governess). And yet we would know very little, only the elements of what would become a period mannerism that Trakl's poems elude by virtue of their anterior origin: they are not intended as literary performances, or demonstrations of belonging to a literary circle, current movement, or cultural situation of any kind. This may be one obstacle, in fact, of coming to Trakl for the first time in the twenty-first century, over a hundred years after his poems entered the public between book covers—his influence is so extensive and deep, so melted into what poetry would become in the twentieth century—from his immediate followers in Expressionism, Futurism, and Surrealism, then across the ocean and expanse of time to midcentury American poets (Robert Bly, James Wright) to a younger generation (Franz Wright, Gregory Orr, Jay Hopler)—that when one picks up Trakl now, he seems to have been indelibly influenced by... well, by Trakl.

Every translator of Trakl creates their own Traklwelt, as they find their way through the sonorities and images which fall and follow one from the other like a kaleidoscope's turning permutations of colored glass. (This often entails choosing which of the several versions of any given poem to translate.) Daniele Pantano's Traklwelt includes all the poems of the two published volumes, *Gedichte* (1913) and the posthumous *Sebastian im Traum* (1915)—minus the prose poem "Transformation of Evil" that appears in the later book—plus twelve additional poems published in *Der Brenner* (1913-15) that comprise the final sequence and crowning achievement (from "In Hellbrun" to "Grodek" in this volume). While many collections of Trakl end with his powerful final poem "Grodek," that he wrote in response to the psychic wounding in 1914 at the battle of Grodek, Pantano has chosen to cap his translation with the first version of an earlier poem, "Three Ponds in Hellbrun" (1909), which rings the range of tensions in Trakl, of an idyllic vision shot through with agony and death wish. With its three "panels" that lift like the heavy lids of his nighttime wanderer in "The Sun," it follows the sweep of the poet's imaginative emotional arc, from singing the "joyful world" of "smiling innocence" to "the mysterious face of the Sphinx, / On which my heart wishes to bleed out."

The strains of melancholy, gloom, unsettling restlessness; the wandering exploring eye of visual otherworldliness that sees familiar environs in strange light and disturbing undertones; such moods as arise from Trakl's poems have long beckoned artists in other media, from composers Anton Webern, Paul Hindemith, Thea Musgrave to heavy black metal bands, from Hermann Nitsch's Orgies Mysteries theater to Anselm Kiefer's canvases. Pantano's translation also follows his own individual interaction and collaboration with Trakl's *oeuvre* in a most intriguing conceptual work, *Orakl* (Black Lawrence, 2017), a kind of *Trakl-dex* that alphabetizes Trakl's body of work by the first word of each and every line, in order to unweave and reconstitute the dynamic of uncanny drift and centripetal force we experience in the stichic juxtapositions of Trakl's verse forms. With such experimental book-length work, Pantano has joined other contemporary poets, such as Jaime Luis Huenún (*Puerto Trakl,* 2001) and Christian Hawkey (*Ventrakl,* 2017) in channeling Trakl's journeying through silence, exile, mystery, and difficult lyric speech, turbid, hallucinatory, and revelatory by turns. Now Pantano joins a host of esteemed translators (Bly & Wright, Daniel Simko, Alexander Stillmark, Robert Firmage, James Reidel, Stephen Tapscott, Will Stone) who have dedicated their knowledge and intuition to revisioning Traklwelt for Anglophone readers. Some of these translators, like Pantano, are poets first, others scholars—they all have something to contribute. But when a poet from one place and time translates another poet from another place and time, we are dropped into a kind of nuclear reactor that generates new energy by virtue of a splitting:

we don't get Trakl (he resides in the German language of the early twentieth century), and we don't get Pantano, either (he's melted into Traklwelt)—we get something like *Traktano*. This is T.S. Eliot's notion of tradition and individual talent turned in on itself, in which the past becomes newly understandable when it joins the contemporary—in fact, we only ever understand the past by virtue of where we're standing now; and because that's always changing, the past is always changing, too. One implication for translation—that participation in poetry's "realms of gold" (Keats) has no time zone other than the simultaneous—rises up rich and realized in Pantano's sensitive and expert translations of Trakl.

How should one read Trakl? Some readers have sensed that the poems teem with symbol-crafting; that the landscapes, objects, and colors that appear in various combinations and ever-shifting permutations comprise a network of meanings, albeit ambiguous, that indicate a kind of allegory stretching across the body of work. Others, while intellectually aroused by that notion, find no pattern or code to support such readings: the poems are so supercharged with ambiguity, they remain in some sense *unreadable,* in large part, because they refuse the reading-for-coherence amidst fragments that scholars, who cut their critical teeth on high modernism, routinely exercise. Is there a middle way? Repetitions are so consistently encountered in Trakl's poetry, one does sense their correspondences from poem to poem—but what do they mean? Some readers have preferred to step back from a framework of reference altogether and reside in the work as an extended tone poem or a palette of moods based on the analogy of musical motif. Every reader will have to work this out for themselves, it's part of the adventure of reading Trakl. But I'd recommend first simply slowing down and taking the time to let each image work on you. Exercise pause at the end of each clause. Absorb its mood; tune in, feel it. Then add the next one; let them interfuse. Continue, take your time. This is not a poetry of scrolling or streaming; it's a constructed space of emotional dimensions established through poetic montage.

Yeats wrote that one of poetry's functions as a primal art form is to make pictures in the mind. And Trakl's poems are particularly cinematic; often each line in a poem by Trakl is a unit of the image; and the poem unfolds as a constructed sequence of images (visual, aural, olfactory, tactile)—the feeling of the poem is not in the rhythmic orchestration of syntax and rhetoric, but rather in the stepped movement from image (line) to image (line). The poems don't sweep you along; they drop you into a space where you experience a sensorium. Trakl referred, in a 1910 letter, to this mode of writing as his "pictorial manner which forges together four separate image-parts in four lines of a stanza into a single impression." (If there were a way to do that in a poem without necessarily enacting the temporality built into language, Trakl, one might feel, would have practiced it). Of course, the art of the poetic line as it corresponds to the image, or the statement (the clause), was widespread in practice—it's an element of classical form. Trakl's innovation was to pit adjacent lines with different emotional pitches against each other, to generate the tension of an expressive contradiction that marks the turmoil inside him. What unifies the poem, then? Readers of Trakl feel the unity of a sensibility whose tensions seem as real as the world. (This feel for contrasts caught in parallel constructions will last after Trakl stops working with rhymed quatrains.) Pantano, who gives us a clean sharp rendering of the Trakl poem, is particularly good at honing each stave of a Trakl composition (he may have developed this feel for Trakl in his work ten years earlier on the long abcedarian of *Orakl*); he translates Trakl into English with the intimacy of the Austrian poet's shadow.

Much has been written about Trakl's *declinism,* his sense that the modern world of the nineteen-teens was in a stage of irrevocable social falling, cultural decay, and moral degradation. And this historical diagnosis is both gestured towards explicitly, and filters into his poetic figuration. While Oswald Spengler's influential *Decline of the West* (1918) did not appear until four years after Trakl's death, that work was nonetheless an intellectual expression of a cultural mood general across Europe at the time (very *zeitgeisty*). The influence of Dostoevsky and Nietzsche has been noted, as well as Kierkegaard, these latter two philosophers seeking a way out of the ethical binds and moral ruins of a Christian Occident. Thinking about major thinkers that created the culture Trakl was vibrating in, it's intriguing that one doesn't find much mention of Freud in connection to the poet; he appears to have been oblivious, impervious, or indifferent to the new science of psychoanalysis. But keep in mind that Freud's *Interpretation of Dreams* (1899) was the groundbreaking study in which Freud peered into the dome of his own dreamworld, where landscapes, figures, objects and colors were found to be indeterminate if suggestive correlatives of waking states, yet without any systematic symbology or set values: dreamsigns—polysemic, layered, contingent, in flux—constantly change in relation to the emotional circumstances and situations of the subject. This seems like a good description of Traklwelt, where traum (*dream,* from the German) and trauma (*wound,* from the Greek) are joined in an ongoing twisting psychic braid. There are recurring set pieces (moors, castles, lakes, forests, village outskirts); set figures (hunters, monks, shepherds, fishermen); alter-egos (Elis, Helian, Sebastian, Kaspar Hauser); the actual environs that Trakl moved through (Salzburg, Innsbruck, Hellbrun); the appearance and reappearance of the figure of the sister and the wanderer; and there is the ever-shifting mood, from soft peacefulness to harsh affliction. Is there a coherent narrative that holds it altogether?

Two minutes on the internet will deliver all the basic trappings of the life story and indicate why Trakl has inspired a kind of cult readership, however central a role he plays in the big story of European modernism: an unusually intimate, if not incestuous, relationship with his sister Grete; early drug use and addiction (his mother was an opium addict); paranoia, depression, fears of mental depravity and madness; tormenting guilt, sustained melancholia, horrifying experiences in the battle of Grodek; attempted suicide, death by overdose. Then there's the self-portrait (painted in Innsbruck in 1913) that nails a viewer in place with the power of a pre-modern tribal mask—deep greens and ochres, with red rimming the eyes and striping the spade-shaped nose: the image of a soul made sick by modern society, a body grown hostile to its hostile environment. And there are the magnetic photographs of Trakl—the eyes on fire, the nose flaring out nostril broad, the lips delicate, the short electric scalp; a smoldering sensitivity; the image of punk *avant la note,* but of anguish, not anger.

Close readers of the poetry, however, may experience something in the work itself that's more complicated than the sensationalism of the tragic life story. *Wahnsinn,* the German word for "madness," is a compound substantive, the first part of which, *Wahn,* means "delusion, delirium," and the second, *Sinn,* means "sense, signification, meaning, purpose." Madness is thus, *in the poetry,* a different embodiment of sense, of meaningfulness. (In the 1950s, in poetry, it was part of a "revolution of the word" aimed at opposing what was called "consensus reality.") It may be from Nietzsche that Trakl picked up the feeling of madness as both symptom of cultural degeneration and source of creativity (the latter arising in response to the former). Whether or not Trakl really suffered from a rising schizophrenia he was diagnosed with, we'll never know, though it is clear from his letters that he suffered great mental distress. (He quite probably had a bipolar disorder.) The madness or derangement or delirium readers often find in his poems—irrationalism, fragmentation, swirling vertiginous mental states of agitation followed by sudden perceptive clarities of peace: these are, in some profound sense, expressions not of fevered madness but a very troubled sanity, if not a sanitized ideation of it. The sanity of Traklwelt is there, beyond the effects of poetry, in the vision, which is not the distortions of insanity, but a manifestation of the visionary faculty that, for example, allows Edvard Munch (born a generation earlier) to see a fallen tree in the forest as a beam of light: a non-dualistic vision that, in Trakl, sees the interdependent co-arising of good and evil; that connects those states of inner peace, harmony in regenerating nature, nurturing elemental softness to the feelings of foreboding, lament, deterioration, menace, even violence. It is, in a sense, a kind of poetic bipolarism (and the poet's genius to gain some formal control over his inner state): an emotional and imagistic spinning without a grounding point of equilibrium; the self provides no axis—does it ever, really? These aspects, qualities, presences, shifting moods exist, in the poems, side-by-side, juxtaposed, layered, one on top of the other, to create what Pound called "an emotional and intellectual complex in an instant of time"—the image. In Trakl, this complex is the image-*effect* of the whole poem, a complex sound we hear and hold as a dark crystal in our mind, and turn and turn in the mind's light.

Rainer Maria Rilke, a most sensitive reader of Trakl, makes the point even more pointed, hearing in the poetry the very dynamic that would animate his own verse, where "the falling [in Trakl] is the pretext for the most continuous ascension. In the history of the poem, Trakl's books are important contributions to the liberation of the poetic image."

The techniques of fragmentation and juxtaposition associated with the advent of modernism, a kind of technology of the image, as evident in the films of Eisenstein as in the verbal and plastic arts of a European avant-garde, are actually ancient, pre-literary structures of storytelling we find in the anonymous folk ballads. And it is in the ballad stanza, especially the cross-rhymed and bracket-rhymed quatrains, that we find Trakl writing his earliest poems (up to about 1911). While borrowing something of the pre-modern folk ballad's mise-en-scène, located in the country, in spaces outside of human concentration, Trakl liberated the image both from the later cultivations of the analytical, and from its more primal function in communal storytelling. Trakl's ballad quatrains hold on to song forms, and the temporal syntactic structures of parallelism, but let go of narrative *per se*—the poems don't tell stories that way. In Trakl, the formal DNA of the poem had evolved; image came forward and stood in the ground of idea; image became ikon of being.

It may be that for twenty-first century readers, the artistic context for Trakl's accomplishment is less apprehensible going back to Expressionism, the dominant artistic movement in Europe between the two world wars, and more familiar if one looks closer to home, to the postwar avant-garde non-narrative filmmaking of an artist such as Stan Brakhage (himself very much influenced by modern poets such as Pound, who innovated with the poetic image): "Imagine an eye unruled by man-made laws of perspective, an eye unprejudiced by compositional logic, an eye which does not respond to the name of everything but which must know each object encountered in life through an adventure of perception. How many colors are there in a field of grass to the crawling baby unaware of 'Green'? How many rainbows can light create for the untutored eye? How aware of variations in heat waves can that eye be? Imagine a world alive with incomprehensible objects and shimmering with an endless variety of movement and innumerable gradations of color. Imagine a world before the 'beginning was the word.'" (*Metaphors on Vision*)

Who sees such objects, this movement, these colors? Readers habituated to poetry as a form of lyric self-dramatization might be startled at the dearth of the first person in Trakl, the way the speaker in his poems is a kind of transparent eye, seeing all in its heightened omniscient super-vision. Dynamics of self-reflection open more as he goes. The first breakthrough is the poem "De Profundis," in *Poems* (1913) where we encounter Trakl speaking in a voice we hear most explicitly as his own. (Ironically, it's also a poem, by virtue of its title, that readers hear echoing Rimbaud; both poets are working in allusive connection to Psalm 130.) The second is "Helian," a stunning longer poem that anchors the 1913 volume; here the full range of Trakl's instrument is sounded, the infernal fuses with the sublime most convincingly, and many of the elements of Traklwelt are pulled together for future work. It would be a tragically curtailed horizon.

The narrative of the life veers from crisis to crisis, growing instability, deepening fears of mental plunging. We might read the poems developing in the opposite direction, however, from immersive, if not hermetic, subjectivities to opening perceptive objectivity. This movement culminates in the posthumous sequence (1914-15) of about twelve poems (thirteen if you include both versions of "Lament") that builds as it moves through sacred forests into the "bare gate of the slaughterhouse" on to a "salty sea of misery" in sleep, a "torn night" purified by fire, and evening figures of "dead heroes" and gleaming stars "above the broken bones of men." The visionary madness of Trakl, his *Wahnsinn*, meets the world's madness in the quotidian hell and *realia* of the Great War. (Pantano's construction of the sequence departs from the publishing record by displacing the penultimate poem, "In the East"—another ferocious poem about the war, with its famous last line, "Wild wolves broke through the gate"—with a recent discovery of a fugitive poem, "Hölderlin," which praises the Romantic poet's "noble head... darkened / In the luster and grief of its beauty / By madness...") In his final poem, "Grodek," that evokes the horror of a battle in which the Austrian army was badly defeated in 1914, human savagery is marked in its counterweight with Trakl's visionary sanity. As Trakl's cry gives voice to the "shattered mouths" of "dying warriors," and the sister's shadow one last time "reels through the silent grove," Trakl hears "the dark flutes of autumn sound softly in the reeds." As he looks up to the "brazen altars" of the heavens, "an immense pain feeds the spirit's hot flame," and he sees, in his mind's final casting, "the unborn descendants," that is, the grandchildren. In his greatest agony, on the threshold of his death, Trakl looked to the future with the sanity of Brecht, and cried for us, and for those who will come after. No deeper sanity or humanity can be found in our poetry.

Joshua Weiner
Truro, MA
July 21, 2025

Nocturne

111 POEMS BY
GEORG TRAKL

Poems

For my children Fiona Katharina and Giacomo Daniele
And for Paula, who knows how to read all the silences...

— dp

DIE RABEN

Über den schwarzen Winkel hasten
Am Mittag die Raben mit hartem Schrei.
Ihr Schatten streift an der Hirschkuh vorbei
Und manchmal sieht man sie mürrisch rasten.

O wie sie die braune Stille stören,
In der ein Acker sich verzückt,
Wie ein Weib, das schwere Ahnung berückt,
Und manchmal kann man sie keifen hören

Um ein Aas, das sie irgendwo wittern,
Und plötzlich richten nach Nord sie den Flug
Und schwinden wie ein Leichenzug
In Lüften, die von Wollust zittern.

THE RAVENS

Above the black patch hurry
The ravens at midday with their harsh caw.
Their shadows streak past the doe
And sometimes you see them in fretful rest.

O how they disturb the brown silence,
In which a field sends itself into ecstasy,
Like a woman burdened by a dire portent,
And sometimes you can hear them fret

Over carrion they smell is somewhere,
And suddenly they point their flight northward
And trickle away like a funeral cortège
Into air that shivers with rapture.

DIE JUNGE MAGD

Ludwig von Ficker zugeeignet

1

Oft am Brunnen, wenn es dämmert,
Sieht man sie verzaubert stehen
Wasser schöpfen, wenn es dämmert.
Eimer auf und nieder gehen.

In den Buchen Dohlen flattern
Und sie gleichet einem Schatten.
Ihre gelben Haare flattern
Und im Hofe schrein die Ratten.

Und umschmeichelt von Verfalle
Senkt sie die entzundenen Lider.
Dürres Gras neigt im Verfalle
Sich zu ihren Füßen nieder.

2

Stille schafft sie in der Kammer
Und der Hof liegt längst verödet.
Im Hollunder vor der Kammer
Kläglich eine Amsel flötet.

Silbern schaut ihr Bild im Spiegel
Fremd sie an im Zwielichtscheine
Und verdämmert fahl im Spiegel
Und ihr graut vor seiner Reine.

Traumhaft singt ein Knecht im Dunkel
Und sie starrt von Schmerz geschüttelt.
Röte träufelt durch das Dunkel.
Jäh am Tor der Südwind rüttelt.

THE YOUNG MAID

Dedicated to Ludwig von Ficker

1

Often by the well at dusk,
You see her standing spellbound
Drawing water at dusk.
Buckets plunge up and down.

In the beeches jackdaws flutter
And she is like a shadow.
Her yellow hair flutters
And rats scream in the yard.

And coaxed by abasement
She lowers her inflamed eyelids.
Parched grass in abasement
Kneels at her feet.

2

She works to herself in the cell
And the yard lies long deserted.
In the elderberry before her cell
A blackbird trills piteously.

Her image peers at her in the mirror
Strange, silvery in the twilight-gleam
And then pales to nothing in the mirror
And she shudders before its purity.

Dreaming, a stablehand sings in the dark
And she stares shaken with pain.
Red trickles down through the dark.
Suddenly the south wind rattles the gate.

3

Nächstens übern kahlen Anger
Gaukelt sie in Fieberträumen.
Mürrisch greint der Wind im Anger
Und der Mond lauscht aus den Bäumen.

Balde rings die Sterne bleichen
Und ermattet von Beschwerde
Wächsern ihre Wangen bleichen.
Fäulnis wittert aus der Erde.

Traurig rauscht das Rohr im Tümpel
Und sie friert in sich gekauert.
Fern ein Hahn kräht. Übern Tümpel
Hart und grau der Morgen schauert.

4

In der Schmiede dröhnt der Hammer
Und sie huscht am Tor vorüber.
Glührot schwingt der Knecht den Hammer
Und sie schaut wie tot hinüber.

Wie im Traum trifft sie ein Lachen;
Und sie taumelt in die Schmiede,
Scheu geduckt vor seinem Lachen,
Wie der Hammer hart und rüde.

Hell versprühn im Raum die Funken
Und mit hilfloser Geberde
Hascht sie nach den wilden Funken
Und sie stürzt betäubt zur Erde.

5

Schmächtig hingestreckt im Bette
Wacht sie auf voll süßem Bangen
Und sie sieht ihr schmutzig Bette
Ganz von goldnem Licht verhangen,

3

At night above the barren meadow
She sways in feverish dreams.
The wind whines morosely in the meadow
And the moon eavesdrops from the trees.

Soon all around the stars grow pale
And weakened by her protests
Her cheeks turn waxen and pale.
Foulness rises from the earth.

The grieving reeds rustle in the pond
And crouched together she freezes.
Far away a cock cries. Across the pond
Morning shivers hard and gray.

4

In the forge pounds a hammer
And she slips past the gate.
Red-hot the stablehand swings his hammer
And as though dead she glances over.

As in a dream she's met by laughter;
And she staggers into the forge,
Cringing at his laughter,
Like the hammer hard and coarse.

Through the room spray blazing sparks
And with helpless gestures
She chases after the wild sparks
And falls overcome to the ground.

5

Stretched out frail upon the bed
She wakes full of sweet terror
And she sees her filthy bed
In a great cloud of golden light,

Die Reseden dort am Fenster
Und den bläulich hellen Himmel.
Manchmal trägt der Wind ans Fenster
Einer Glocke zag Gebimmel.

Schatten gleiten übers Kissen,
Langsam schlägt die Mittagsstunde
Und sie atmet schwer im Kissen
Und ihr Mund gleicht einer Wunde.

6

Abends schweben blutige Linnen,
Wolken über stummen Wäldern,
Die gehüllt in schwarze Linnen.
Spatzen lärmen auf den Feldern.

Und sie liegt ganz weiß im Dunkel.
Unterm Dach verhaucht ein Girren.
Wie ein Aas in Busch und Dunkel
Fliegen ihren Mund umschwirren.

Traumhaft klingt im braunen Weiler
Nach ein Klang von Tanz und Geigen,
Schwebt ihr Antlitz durch den Weiler,
Weht ihr Haar in kahlen Zweigen.

The mignonettes there at the window
And the blue bright sky.
Sometimes the wind carries to the window
The timid ringing of a bell.

Shadows glide across the pillow,
The noon hour strikes slowly
And she breathes hard upon the pillow
And her mouth is like a wound.

6

At evening drift bloody linens,
Clouds over silent forests
Draped in black linens.
Sparrows clamor in the fields.

And she lies utterly white in the dark.
Beneath the eaves a cooing fades.
Like a carrion in the underbrush and dark
Flies buzz around her mouth.

Dreamlike a sound in the brown village,
An echo of dancing and violins,
Her face floats through the village,
Her hair catches in the bare branches.

ROMANZE ZUR NACHT

Einsamer unterm Sternenzelt
Geht durch die stille Mitternacht.
Der Knab aus Träumen wirr erwacht,
Sein Antlitz grau im Mond verfällt.

Die Närrin weint mit offnem Haar
Am Fenster, das vergittert starrt.
Im Teich vorbei auf süßer Fahrt
Ziehn Liebende sehr wunderbar.

Der Mörder lächelt bleich im Wein,
Die Kranken Todesgrausen packt.
Die Nonne betet wund und nackt
Vor des Heilands Kreuzespein.

Die Mutter leis' im Schlafe singt.
Sehr friedlich schaut zur Nacht das Kind
Mit Augen, die ganz wahrhaft sind.
Im Hurenhaus Gelächter klingt.

Beim Talglicht drunt' im Kellerloch
Der Tote malt mit weißer Hand
Ein grinsend Schweigen an die Wand.
Der Schläfer flüstert immer noch.

A ROMANCE TO NIGHT

Under the starred canvas the lonely man
Walks through the silent midnight.
The boy wakes wild from dreams,
His ruined face gray in the moon.

At the window whose stare is barred
The clowness weeps with unbound hair.
Wonderfully lovers on a sweet journey
Drift by on the pond.

The murderer simpers pale in the wine,
The horror of death seizes the sick.
Sore and naked the nun prays
Before the Savior's agony on the cross.

The mother sings softly in her sleep.
So tranquil the child peers into the night
With eyes that are utterly honest.
The whorehouse peals with laughter.

By the suet-light in the cellar pit
The dead man with white hand
Paints a grinning silence on the wall.
The sleeper still whispers.

IM ROTEN LAUBWERK VOLL GUITARREN...

Im roten Laubwerk voll Guitarren
Der Mädchen gelbe Haare wehen
Am Zaun, wo Sonnenblumen stehen.
Durch Wolken fährt ein goldner Karren.

In brauner Schatten Ruh verstummen
Die Alten, die sich blöd umschlingen.
Die Waisen süß zur Vesper singen.
In gelben Dünsten Fliegen summen.

Am Bache waschen noch die Frauen.
Die aufgehängten Linnen wallen.
Die Kleine, die mir lang gefallen,
Kommt wieder durch das Abendgrauen.

Vom lauen Himmel Spatzen stürzen
In grüne Löcher voll Verwesung.
Dem Hungrigen täuscht vor Genesung
Ein Duft von Brot und herben Würzen.

IN RED LEAVES FULL OF GUITARS...

In red leaves full of guitars
The yellow tresses of girls flutter
By the fence where sunflowers grow.
A golden tumbrel wheels through the clouds.

The elders in a peace of brown shadow
Become silent and hug each other like fools.
Orphans sing sweetly at vespers.
Flies buzz in yellow palls.

At the stream the women still wash.
The hanging linens sail.
The girlchild I long fell for
Comes again through the evening gray.

Sparrows plunge from balmy skies
Into green voids filled with rot.
A bread smell and pungent spice
Cheats the hungry one of recovery.

MUSIK IM MIRABELL

2. Fassung

Ein Brunnen singt. Die Wolken stehn
Im klaren Blau, die weißen, zarten.
Bedächtig stille Menschen gehn
Am Abend durch den alten Garten.

Der Ahnen Marmor ist ergraut.
Ein Vogelzug streift in die Weiten.
Ein Faun mit toten Augen schaut
Nach Schatten, die ins Dunkel gleiten.

Das Laub fällt rot vom alten Baum
Und kreist herein durchs offne Fenster.
Ein Feuerschein glüht auf im Raum
Und malet trübe Angstgespenster.

Ein weißer Fremdling tritt ins Haus.
Ein Hund stürzt durch verfallene Gänge.
Die Magd löscht eine Lampe aus,
Das Ohr hört nachts Sonatenklänge.

MUSIC IN MIRABELL

2ⁿᵈ Version

A fountain lilts. In the clear blue
Are the clouds, white, wisping.
Silent people walk in measures
In the evening through the old garden.

The ancestral marble has grayed.
A line of birds slips into the distance.
A faun with dead eyes stares
After shadows gliding into the dark.

Leaves drop red from the ancient tree
And whirl in through the open window.
A firelight blazes in the room
And paints panic's grim specters.

A white stranger enters the building.
A dog lunges along ruined paths.
The maid snuffs out a lamp,
The ear hears night's sonata notes.

MELANCHOLIE DES ABENDS

– Der Wald, der sich verstorben breitet –
Und Schatten sind um ihn, wie Hecken.
Das Wild kommt zitternd aus Verstecken,
Indes ein Bach ganz leise gleitet

Und Farnen folgt und alten Steinen
Und silbern glänzt aus Laubgewinden.
Man hört ihn bald in schwarzen Schlünden –
Vielleicht, daß auch schon Sterne scheinen.

Der dunkle Plan scheint ohne Maßen,
Verstreute Dörfer, Sumpf und Weiher,
Und etwas täuscht dir vor ein Feuer.
Ein kalter Glanz huscht über Straßen.

Am Himmel ahnet man Bewegung,
Ein Heer von wilden Vögeln wandern
Nach jenen Ländern, schönen, andern.
Es steigt und sinkt des Rohres Regung.

EVENING MELANCHOLY

—The forest, which unfolds itself decayed—
And shadows enclose it, like hedgerows.
The deer comes tremulous from its lairs,
While a brook flows by in silence

And follows ferns and old stones
And glimmers silvery from tangled leaves.
Soon you hear it in black defiles—
That stars are already perhaps appearing too.

The dark plain appears without end,
Scattered villages, fen and pond,
And something you mistake for a fire.
A cold luster darts across streets.

You sense commotion in the sky,
A host of wild birds migrating
To those lands, beautiful, different.
There rises and falls the motion of the reeds.

WINTERDÄMMERUNG

An Max von Esterle

Schwarze Himmel von Metall.
Kreuz in roten Stürmen wehen
Abends hungertolle Krähen
Über Parken gram und fahl.

Im Gewölk erfriert ein Strahl;
Und vor Satans Flüchen drehen
Jene sich im Kreis und gehen
Nieder siebenfach an Zahl.

In Verfaultem süß und schal
Lautlos ihre Schnäbel mähen.
Häuser dräu'n aus stummen Nähen;
Helle im Theatersaal.

Kirchen, Brücken und Spital
Grauenvoll im Zwielicht stehen.
Blutbefleckte Linnen blähen
Segel sich auf dem Kanal.

WINTER TWILIGHT

To Max von Esterle

Black skies of metal.
Criss-cross in red storms blow
Hunger mad crows at dusk
Above parks in grief and pale.

A light shaft freezes in the clouds;
And before Satan's curses
They circle and descend
Sevenfold in number.

In sweet and stale rot
Soundless their bills shear.
Houses loom from mute threats;
Brightness in the theater.

Churches, bridges and hospitals
Stand ghastly in the twilight.
Blood-spattered linens billow
Sails upon the canal.

RONDEL

Verflossen ist das Gold der Tage,
Des Abends braun und blaue Farben:
Des Hirten sanfte Flöten starben
Des Abends blau und braune Farben
Verflossen ist das Gold der Tage.

RONDEL

Fleeting is the gold of days,
The evening's brown and blue colors:
The shepherd's gentle flutes died
The evening's blue and brown colors
Fleeting is the gold of days.

FRAUENSEGEN

Schreitest unter deinen Frau'n
Und du lächelst oft beklommen:
Sind so bange Tage kommen.
Weiß verblüht der Mohn am Zaun.

Wie dein Leib so schön geschwellt
Golden reift der Wein am Hügel.
Ferne glänzt des Weihers Spiegel
Und die Sense klirrt im Feld.

In den Büschen rollt der Tau,
Rot die Blätter niederfließen.
Seine liebe Frau zu grüßen
Naht ein Mohr dir braun und rauh.

THE BLESSING OF WOMEN

You step among your womankind
And often smile in anguish:
Such anxious days are coming.
By the fence the poppy wilts white.

Like your belly so beautifully swollen
Grapes ripen to gold on the hill.
The pond's mirror flashes from afar
And the scythe clashes in the field.

The dew beads in the bushes,
The leaves run down red.
To greet his darling wife, a Moor
Appears before you brown and raw.

DIE SCHÖNE STADT

Alte Plätze sonnig schweigen.
Tief in Blau und Gold versponnen
Traumhaft hasten sanfte Nonnen
Unter schwüler Buchen Schweigen.

Aus den braun erhellten Kirchen
Schaun des Todes reine Bilder,
Großer Fürsten schöne Schilder.
Kronen schimmern in den Kirchen.

Rösser tauchen aus dem Brunnen.
Blütenkrallen drohn aus Bäumen.
Knaben spielen wirr von Träumen
Abends leise dort am Brunnen.

Mädchen stehen an den Toren,
Schauen scheu ins farbige Leben.
Ihre feuchten Lippen beben
Und sie warten an den Toren.

Zitternd flattern Glockenklänge,
Marschtakt hallt und Wacherufen.
Fremde lauschen auf den Stufen.
Hoch im Blau sind Orgelklänge.

Helle Instrumente singen.
Durch der Gärten Blätterrahmen
Schwirrt das Lachen schöner Damen.
Leise junge Mütter singen.

Heimlich haucht an blumigen Fenstern
Duft von Weihrauch, Teer und Flieder.
Silbern flimmern müde Lider
Durch die Blumen an den Fenstern.

THE BEAUTIFUL CITY

Old squares keep sunlit silence.
Spun in deep blue and gold
Nuns hurry like silk in a dream
Amid an airless beech tree silence.

From the brown-lit churches
Peer death's untainted tableaus,
Mighty princes' beautiful armor.
Crowns gleam in the churches.

Horses plunge from the fountain.
Clawed blossoms loom in the trees.
In the bewilderment of dreams boys play
In the evening softly there at the fountain.

Girls stand in archways,
Shyly staring into a colorful life.
Their moist lips tremble
And they wait in archways.

A quake of church chimes upswells,
Marching drums and the shouting of the guard.
Strangers listen on the steps.
Up into the blue organs swell.

Bright instruments sing.
Through gardened frames of leaves
Twirls the laughter of fine ladies.
Softly young mothers sing.

Sly perfume in flowered windows
Whispers of incense, tar and lilac.
Tired eyelids flicker silvery
Through the flowers in the windows.

IN EINEM VERLASSENEN ZIMMER

Fenster, bunte Blumenbeeten,
Eine Orgel spielt herein.
Schatten tanzen an Tapeten,
Wunderlich ein toller Reihn.

Lichterloh die Büsche wehen
Und ein Schwarm von Mücken schwingt.
Fern im Acker Sensen mähen
Und ein altes Wasser singt.

Wessen Atem kommt mich kosen?
Schwalben irre Zeichen ziehn.
Leise fließt im Grenzenlosen
Dort das goldne Waldland hin.

Flammen flackern in den Beeten.
Wirr verzückt der tolle Reihn
An den gelblichen Tapeten.
Jemand schaut zur Tür herein.

Weihrauch duftet süß und Birne
Und es dämmern Glas und Truh.
Langsam beugt die heiße Stirne
Sich den weißen Sternen zu.

IN AN ABANDONED ROOM

Window, brilliant beds of flowers,
An organ comes playing in.
Shadows dance on wallpaper,
A fantastically mad sequence.

Ablaze the bushes waver
And a pulsating swarm of gnats.
On distant fields scythes mow
And an ancient water sings.

Whose breath comes to caress me?
Swallows draw insane signs.
There through boundless space
The golden woodland softly flows.

Flames flicker in the beds.
Enraptured this mad sequence
Scattered on yellowed wallpaper.
Someone gazes through the door.

Sweet smell of incense and pears
And glass and chest in twilight.
Slowly the feverish forehead
Bows to the white stars.

AN DEN KNABEN ELIS

Elis, wenn die Amsel im schwarzen Wald ruft,
Dieses ist dein Untergang.
Deine Lippen trinken die Kühle des blauen Felsenquells.

Laß, wenn deine Stirne leise blutet
Uralte Legenden
Und dunkle Deutung des Vogelflugs.

Du aber gehst mit weichen Schritten in die Nacht,
Die voll purpurner Trauben hängt
Und du regst die Arme schöner im Blau.

Ein Dornenbusch tönt,
Wo deine mondenen Augen sind.
O, wie lange bist, Elis, du verstorben.

Dein Leib ist eine Hyazinthe,
In die ein Mönch die wächsernen Finger taucht.
Eine schwarze Höhle ist unser Schweigen,

Daraus bisweilen ein sanftes Tier tritt
Und langsam die schweren Lider senkt.
Auf deine Schläfen tropft schwarzer Tau,

Das letzte Gold verfallener Sterne.

TO THE BOY ELIS

Elis, when the blackbird calls in the black wood,
This is your doom.
Your lips drink the coolness of the blue rock-spring.

Forsake, when your brow gently bleeds
Ancient legends
And dark readings of the flight of birds.

But with soft steps you walk into the night,
Where crimson grapes hang thick
And you move your arms more beautifully in this blue.

A thorn bush sounds,
Where your moonlike eyes are.
O how long, Elis, have you been deceased.

Your body is a hyacinth,
Into which a monk dips the waxen fingers.
Our silence is a black cave,

From which sometimes a gentle beast emerges
And slowly lowers its heavy eyelids.
Black dew drips upon your temples,

The last gold of fallen stars.

DER GEWITTERABEND

O die roten Abendstunden!
Flimmernd schwankt am offenen Fenster
Weinlaub wirr ins Blau gewunden,
Drinnen nisten Angstgespenster.

Staub tanzt im Gestank der Gossen.
Klirrend stößt der Wind in Scheiben.
Einen Zug von wilden Rossen
Blitze grelle Wolken treiben.

Laut zerspringt der Weiherspiegel.
Möven schrein am Fensterrahmen.
Feuerreiter sprengt vom Hügel
Und zerschellt im Tann zu Flammen.

Kranke kreischen im Spitale.
Bläulich schwirrt der Nacht Gefieder.
Glitzernd braust mit einem Male
Regen auf die Dächer nieder.

TEMPEST EVE

O the red hours of evening!
Flitting, wavering at the open window
Grape leaves scatter whirling into blue,
Inside fear's ghosts huddle.

Dust spins in the reek of gutters.
The wind pounds the rattling panes.
A procession of wild horses
Driven by flashes of blazing clouds.

The mirror pond shatters with a bang.
Gulls shriek by the window frames.
A burning rider explodes from the hillside
And bursts into flames in the pine forest.

The sick scream in the hospital.
Bluely the night's plumage whorls.
All at once glittering rain
Rushes down upon the roofs.

ABENDMUSE

Ans Blumenfenster wieder kehrt des Kirchturms Schatten
Und Goldnes. Die heiße Stirn verglüht in Ruh und Schweigen.
Ein Brunnen fällt im Dunkel von Kastanienzweigen –
Da fühlst du: es ist gut! in schmerzlichem Ermatten.

Der Markt ist leer von Sommerfrüchten und Gewinden.
Einträchtig stimmt der Tore schwärzliches Gepränge.
In einem Garten tönen sanften Spieles Klänge,
Wo Freunde nach dem Mahle sich zusammenfinden.

Des weißen Magiers Märchen lauscht die Seele gerne.
Rund saust das Korn, das Mäher nachmittags geschnitten.
Geduldig schweigt das harte Leben in den Hütten;
Der Kühe linden Schlaf bescheint die Stalllaterne.

Von Lüften trunken sinken balde ein die Lider
Und öffnen leise sich zu fremden Sternenzeichen.
Endymion taucht aus dem Dunkel alter Eichen
Und beugt sich über trauervolle Wasser nieder.

EVENING MUSE

The church tower's shadow returns to the flower window
And something gold. The burning brow dies down in calm and
    silence.
A fountain falls in the darkness of chestnut branches—
Then you feel: it is good! in painful exhaustion.

The market is empty of summer fruit and garlands.
Peaceful the union of the gates' blackish splendor.
In a garden the notes of a gentle game are sounding,
Where friends come together after their meal.

Gladly the soul listens to the white magician's fairy tales.
Wheat rustles all around, cut by reapers in the afternoon.
Patiently the hard life keeps silent in the shacks;
The stable lamp shines upon the cattle's balmy sleep.

Drunk with air eyelids soon sink inward
And open softly to strange constellations.
Endymion emerges from the dark of ancient oaks
And bows down low over mournful waters.

TRAUM DES BÖSEN

1. Fassung

Verhallend eines Gongs braungoldne Klänge –
Ein Liebender erwacht in schwarzen Zimmern
Die Wang' an Flammen, die im Fenster flimmern.
Am Strome blitzen Segel, Masten, Stränge.

Ein Mönch, ein schwangres Weib dort im Gedränge.
Guitarren klimpern, rote Kittel schimmern.
Kastanien schwül in goldnem Glanz verkümmern;
Schwarz ragt der Kirchen trauriges Gepränge.

Aus bleichen Masken schaut der Geist des Bösen.
Ein Platz verdämmert grauenvoll und düster;
Am Abend regt auf Inseln sich Geflüster.

Des Vogelfluges wirre Zeichen lesen
Aussätzige, die zur Nacht vielleicht verwesen.
Im Park erblicken zitternd sich Geschwister.

DREAM OF EVIL

1ˢᵗ Version

Fading of a gong's brown-golden sounds—
A lover stirs in black rooms
His cheeks near flames that flicker in the window.
Sails, masts, ropes flash on the river.

A monk, a pregnant woman there in the crowd.
Guitars strum, red coats shimmer.
Chestnuts waste away in the heavy golden glow;
Black soars the mournful ceremony of churches.

The ghost of evil watches from pale masks.
A square darkens grim and sinister;
At evening a whispering rises on the islands.

Lepers, rotting perhaps that night,
Read confused omens from the flight of birds.
In the park siblings behold each other trembling.

GEISTLICHES LIED

Zeichen, seltne Stickerein
Malt ein flatternd Blumenbeet.
Gottes blauer Odem weht
In den Gartensaal herein,
Heiter ein.
Ragt ein Kreuz im wilden Wein.

Hör' im Dorf sich viele freun,
Gärtner an der Mauer mäht,
Leise eine Orgel geht,
Mischet Klang und goldenen Schein,
Klang und Schein.
Liebe segnet Brot und Wein.

Mädchen kommen auch herein
Und der Hahn zum letzten kräht.
Sacht ein morsches Gitter geht
Und in Rosen Kranz und Reihn,
Rosenreihn
Ruht Maria weiß und fein.

Bettler dort am alten Stein
Scheint verstorben im Gebet,
Sanft ein Hirt vom Hügel geht
Und ein Engel singt im Hain,
Nah im Hain
Kinder in den Schlaf hinein.

SPIRITUAL SONG

A fluttering flowerbed
Paints symbols, rare embroideries.
God's blue breath wafts
Into the garden hall,
Serenely in.
A cross towers in the wild vines.

Hear the villagers rejoicing,
A gardener mows at the wall,
Quietly an organ goes,
Mixing sound and golden light,
Sound and light.
Love blesses bread and wine.

Girls are coming in as well
And the cock crows to the last.
Gently a rotting trellis goes
And in the crown of roses and rows,
Rows of roses
Mary rests pale and delicate.

A beggar there at the ancient stone
Appears to have died in prayer,
Softly from a hill a shepherd goes
And an angel in the grove,
Near in the grove
Sings children to sleep.

IM HERBST

Die Sonnenblumen leuchten am Zaun,
Still sitzen Kranke im Sonnenschein.
Im Acker mühn sich singend die Frau'n,
Die Klosterglocken läuten darein.

Die Vögel sagen dir ferne Mär',
Die Klosterglocken läuten darein.
Vom Hof tönt sanft die Geige her.
Heut keltern sie den braunen Wein.

Da zeigt der Mensch sich froh und lind.
Heut keltern sie den braunen Wein.
Weit offen die Totenkammern sind
Und schön bemalt vom Sonnenschein.

IN AUTUMN

Sunflowers glow along the fence,
The sick sit silent in the sunshine.
Women sing and toil in the field,
Into which cloister bells peal.

The birds tell you faraway tales,
Into which cloister bells peal.
A soft violin sounds from the courtyard.
Today they tread the brown grapes.

Here mankind is joyful and gentle.
Today they tread the brown grapes.
The death chambers are wide open
And beautifully painted by sunshine.

ZU ABEND MEIN HERZ

Am Abend hört man den Schrei der Fledermäuse.
Zwei Rappen springen auf der Wiese.
Der rote Ahorn rauscht.
Dem Wanderer erscheint die kleine Schenke am Weg.
Herrlich schmecken junger Wein und Nüsse.
Herrlich: betrunken zu taumeln in dämmernden Wald.
Durch schwarzes Geäst tönen schmerzliche Glocken.
Auf das Gesicht tropft Tau.

MY HEART AT EVENING

At nightfall you hear the bats shriek.
Two black horses leap across the meadow.
The red maple rustles.
The small inn along the way appears to the traveler.
Delicious the young wine and nuts.
Delicious: to stagger drunk in the darkening forest.
Cruel bells ring through black branches.
Dew drips on the face.

DIE BAUERN

Vorm Fenster tönendes Grün und Rot.
Im schwarzverräucherten, niederen Saal
Sitzen die Knechte und Mägde beim Mahl;
Und sie schenken den Wein und sie brechen das Brot.

Im tiefen Schweigen der Mittagszeit
Fällt bisweilen ein karges Wort.
Die Äcker flimmern in einem fort
Und der Himmel bleiern und weit.

Fratzenhaft flackert im Herd die Glut
Und ein Schwarm von Fliegen summt.
Die Mägde lauschen blöd und verstummt
Und ihre Schläfen hämmert das Blut.

Und manchmal treffen sich Blicke voll Gier,
Wenn tierischer Dunst die Stube durchweht.
Eintönig spricht ein Knecht das Gebet
Und ein Hahn kräht unter der Tür.

Und wieder ins Feld. Ein Grauen packt
Sie oft im tosenden Ährengebraus
Und klirrend schwingen ein und aus
Die Sensen geisterhaft im Takt.

THE PEASANTS

Ringing green and red before the window.
In the low, smoke-blackened hall
Farmhands and maids have begun their meal;
And they pour the wine and break the bread.

From time to time a scant word drops
In the deep silence of noon.
The fields shimmer without end
And the sky leaden and vast.

In the stove a hideous glow of embers
And a swarm of flies buzzes.
The maids listen dumb and mute
And blood pounds in their temples.

And sometimes lustful glances meet
When animal fumes waft through the room.
A farmhand intones the prayer
And a cock crows beneath the door.

And back to the field. A horror often
Seizes them in the raging roar of wheat
And with shrills the scythes swing
Ghostly back and forth in time.

ALLERSEELEN

An Karl Hauer

Die Männlein, Weiblein, traurige Gesellen,
Sie streuen heute Blumen blau und rot
Auf ihre Grüfte, die sich zag erhellen.
Sie tun wie arme Puppen vor dem Tod.

O! wie sie hier voll Angst und Demut scheinen,
Wie Schatten hinter schwarzen Büschen stehn.
Im Herbstwind klagt der Ungebornen Weinen,
Auch sieht man Lichter in der Irre gehn.

Das Seufzen Liebender haucht in Gezweigen
Und dort verwest die Mutter mit dem Kind.
Unwirklich scheinet der Lebendigen Reigen
Und wunderlich zerstreut im Abendwind.

Ihr Leben ist so wirr, voll trüber Plagen.
Erbarm' dich Gott der Frauen Höll' und Qual,
Und dieser hoffnungslosen Todesklagen.
Einsame wandeln still im Sternensaal.

ALL SOULS' DAY

To Karl Hauer

The little men, little women, sad companions,
Today they strew flowers blue and red
On their crypts, which light up shyly.
They move like helpless marionettes before death.

O! how full of fear and lowliness they seem,
Like shadows standing behind black shrubbery.
On the wailing autumn wind the cries of the unborn,
And you see lights that have lost their way.

The sighs of lovers breathe in the branches
And there the mother rots with her child.
The roundelay of the living appears unreal
And strangely scattered in the evening wind.

Their lives are so tangled, full of dreary plagues.
God take pity on these women's hellish agony,
And these hopeless laments for the dead.
The lonely wander quietly in the hall of stars.

MELANCHOLIE

3. Fassung

Bläuliche Schatten. O ihr dunklen Augen,
Die lang mich anschaun im Vorübergleiten.
Guitarrenklänge sanft den Herbst begleiten
Im Garten, aufgelöst in braunen Laugen.

Des Todes ernste Düsternis bereiten
Nymphische Hände, an roten Brüsten saugen
Verfallne Lippen und in schwarzen Laugen
Des Sonnenjünglings feuchte Locken gleiten.

MELANCHOLY

3ʳᵈ Version

Blue shadows. O you dark eyes
That keep staring at me as you glide by.
Strains of a guitar softly accompany autumn
In the garden, dissolved in brown lyes.
Hands of nymphs cause death's
Grave darkness, decayed lips suck
At red breasts and in black lyes
The sun-youth's moist locks float.

SEELE DES LEBENS

Verfall, der weich das Laub umdüstert,
Es wohnt im Wald sein weites Schweigen.
Bald scheint ein Dorf sich geisterhaft zu neigen.
Der Schwester Mund in schwarzen Zweigen flüstert.

Der Einsame wird bald entgleiten,
Vielleicht ein Hirt auf dunklen Pfaden.
Ein Tier tritt leise aus den Baumarkaden,
Indes die Lider sich vor Gottheit weiten.

Der blaue Fluß rinnt schön hinunter,
Gewölke sich am Abend zeigen;
Die Seele auch in engelhaftem Schweigen.
Vergängliche Gebilde gehen unter.

SOUL OF LIFE

Decay that softly darkens the leaves,
Its vast silence lives in the forest.
Soon a village seems to bow like a ghost.
The sister's mouth whispers in black branches.

The lonely one will soon slip away,
Perhaps a shepherd on dark paths.
A beast steps silently from tree arcades,
While the eyelids widen before godship.

The blue river runs down lovely,
Clouds reveal themselves at evening;
The soul too in angelic silence.
Fleeting shapes go down.

VERKLÄRTER HERBST

Gewaltig endet so das Jahr
Mit goldnem Wein und Frucht der Gärten.
Rund schweigen Wälder wunderbar
Und sind des Einsamen Gefährten.

Da sagt der Landmann: Es ist gut.
Ihr Abendglocken lang und leise
Gebt noch zum Ende frohen Mut.
Ein Vogelzug grüßt auf der Reise.

Es ist der Liebe milde Zeit.
Im Kahn den blauen Fluß hinunter
Wie schön sich Bild an Bildchen reiht –
Das geht in Ruh und Schweigen unter.

TRANSFIGURED AUTUMN

Magnificently does the year thus end
With golden wine and fruit of gardens.
All around the forests are gloriously mute
And are the lonely one's companions.

Then the farmer says: It is good.
You evening bells long and soft
In parting lend good spirits.
A line of birds greets on its journey.

It is the tender time of love.
In a boat down the blue river
How beautifully image follows image—
This founders in peace and silence.

WINKEL AM WALD

An Karl Minnich

Braune Kastanien. Leise gleiten die alten Leute
In stilleren Abend; weich verwelken schöne Blätter.
Am Friedhof scherzt die Amsel mit dem toten Vetter,
Angelen gibt der blonde Lehrer das Geleite.

Des Todes reine Bilder schaun von Kirchenfenstern;
Doch wirkt ein blutiger Grund sehr trauervoll und düster.
Das Tor blieb heut verschlossen. Den Schlüssel hat der Küster.
Im Garten spricht die Schwester freundlich mit Gespenstern.

In alten Kellern reift der Wein ins Goldne, Klare.
Süß duften Äpfel. Freude glänzt nicht allzu ferne.
Den langen Abend hören Kinder Märchen gerne;
Auch zeigt sich sanftem Wahnsinn oft das Goldne, Wahre.

Das Blau fließt voll Reseden; in Zimmern Kerzenhelle.
Bescheidenen ist ihre Stätte wohl bereitet.
Den Saum des Walds hinab ein einsam Schicksal gleitet;
Die Nacht erscheint, der Ruhe Engel, auf der Schwelle.

CORNER BY THE FOREST

To Karl Minnich

Brown chestnuts. Old people glide silently
Into the stiller evening; beautiful leaves wither softly.
By the graveyard the blackbird jests with the dead cousin,
The fair-haired teacher guides Angela's walk.

Death's pure images peer from church windows;
But a bloody ground seems very mournful and grim.
The gate remained locked today. The sexton has the key.
In the garden the sister speaks kindly with specters.

In old cellars the wine mellows into the golden, clear.
Sweet fragrance of apples. Joy sheens not very far away.
Children gladly listen to fairy tales through the long evening;
And often the golden and true show themselves to gentle
    madness.

The blue flows full of mignonettes; candlelight in rooms.
The humble find their sites well prepared.
A lonely fate glides down the forest edge;
Night appears, the angel of rest, on the threshold.

IM WINTER

Der Acker leuchtet weiß und kalt.
Der Himmel ist einsam und ungeheuer.
Dohlen kreisen über dem Weiher
Und Jäger steigen nieder vom Wald.

Ein Schweigen in schwarzen Wipfeln wohnt.
Ein Feuerschein huscht aus den Hütten.
Bisweilen schellt sehr fern ein Schlitten
Und langsam steigt der graue Mond.

Ein Wild verblutet sanft am Rain
Und Raben plätschern in blutigen Gossen.
Das Rohr bebt gelb und aufgeschossen.
Frost, Rauch, ein Schritt im leeren Hain.

IN WINTER

The field gleams white and cold.
The sky is lonely and vast.
Jackdaws circle above the pond
And hunters descend from the forest.

A silence dwells in black treetops.
A firelight flashes from the cottages.
Sometimes a sleigh rings in the distance
And slowly the gray moon climbs.

On the ridge a deer bleeds softly to death
And ravens splash in bloody gutters.
Reeds tremble yellow and tall.
Frost, smoke, a footstep in the empty grove.

IN EIN ALTES STAMMBUCH

Immer wieder kehrst du Melancholie,
O Sanftmut der einsamen Seele.
Zu Ende glüht ein goldener Tag.

Demutsvoll beugt sich dem Schmerz der Geduldige
Tönend von Wohllaut und weichem Wahnsinn.
Siehe! es dämmert schon.

Wieder kehrt die Nacht und klagt ein Sterbliches
Und es leidet ein anderes mit.

Schaudernd unter herbstlichen Sternen
Neigt sich jährlich tiefer das Haupt.

INTO AN OLD FAMILY REGISTER

Again and again you return, melancholy,
O gentleness of the lonely soul.
A golden day glows to its end.

The patient one humbly submits to pain,
Resonant with melodious sound and soft madness.
Look! already dusk is falling.

Again night returns and a mortal thing laments
And another suffers with it.

Shuddering beneath autumnal stars
Each year the head bows more deeply.

VERWANDLUNG

2. Fassung

Entlang an Gärten, herbstlich, rotversengt:
Hier zeigt im Stillen sich ein tüchtig Leben.
Des Menschen Hände tragen braune Reben,
Indes der sanfte Schmerz im Blick sich senkt.

Am Abend: Schritte gehn durch schwarzes Land
Erscheinender in roter Buchen Schweigen.
Ein blaues Tier will sich vorm Tod verneigen
Und grauenvoll verfällt ein leer Gewand.

Geruhiges vor einer Schenke spielt,
Ein Antlitz ist berauscht ins Gras gesunken.
Hollunderfrüchte, Flöten weich und trunken,
Resedenduft, der Weibliches umspült.

METAMORPHOSIS

2nd Version

Past gardens, autumnal, singed with red:
Here a capable life shows itself in silence.
The hands of man carry brown vines,
While the gentle pain in his gaze lowers.

At evening: steps come through black land
More clearly in the silence of red beeches.
A blue beast wants to bow before death
And horridly an empty garment decays.

Something calm plays before a tavern,
A face has sunk drunkenly into the grass.
Elderberries, flutes soft and intoxicated,
Scent of mignonettes bathes the female.

KLEINES KONZERT

Ein Rot, das traumhaft dich erschüttert –
Durch deine Hände scheint die Sonne.
Du fühlst dein Herz verrückt vor Wonne
Sich still zu einer Tat bereiten.

In Mittag strömen gelbe Felder.
Kaum hörst du noch der Grillen Singen,
Der Mäher hartes Sensenschwingen.
Einfältig schweigen goldene Wälder.

Im grünen Tümpel glüht Verwesung.
Die Fische stehen still. Gotts Odem
Weckt sacht ein Saitenspiel im Brodem.
Aussätzigen winkt die Flut Genesung.

Geist Dädals schwebt in blauen Schatten,
Ein Duft von Milch in Haselzweigen.
Man hört noch lang den Lehrer geigen,
Im leeren Hof den Schrei der Ratten.

Im Krug an scheußlichen Tapeten
Blühn kühlere Violenfarben.
Im Hader dunkle Stimmung starben,
Narziß im Endakkord von Flöten.

SMALL CONCERT

A red that shakes you like a dream—
The sun shines through your hands.
You feel you heart mad with bliss
Quietly preparing itself for an act.

Yellow fields stream into noon.
You can barely hear the crickets' song,
The harsh swings of the reapers' scythe.
The simple silence of golden forests.

Rot glows in the green pool.
The fish stand still. God's breath
Gently wakes string music in the haze.
The healing flood beckons the lepers.

Daedalus's spirit hovers in blue shadows,
A scent of milk in hazel branches.
You still hear the teacher's lingering fiddle,
The scream of rats in the empty courtyard.

In the tavern on rotten wallpaper
Cooler colors of violet blossom.
Dark voices died in strife,
Narcissus in the final chord of flutes.

MENSCHHEIT

Menschheit vor Feuerschlünden aufgestellt,
Ein Trommelwirbel, dunkler Krieger Stirnen,
Schritte durch Blutnebel; schwarzes Eisen schellt,
Verzweiflung, Nacht in traurigen Gehirnen:
Hier Evas Schatten, Jagd und rotes Geld.
Gewölk, das Licht durchbricht, das Abendmahl.
Es wohnt in Brot und Wein ein sanftes Schweigen
Und jene sind versammelt zwölf an Zahl.
Nachts schrein im Schlaf sie unter Ölbaumzweigen;
Sankt Thomas taucht die Hand ins Wundenmal.

MANKIND

Mankind lined up before fiery gorges,
A rolling drum, black foreheads of warriors,
Footsteps through a fog of blood; black steel echoes,
Despair, night in brains of grief:
Here the shadow of Eve, the hunt and red coins.
Clouds, shot through by light, the Last Supper.
A gentle silence lives in bread and wine
And the assembled are twelve in number.
At night they scream in sleep under olive limbs;
Saint Thomas dips his hand into the stigmata.

DER SPAZIERGANG

1

Musik summt im Gehölz am Nachmittag.
Im Korn sich ernste Vogelscheuchen drehn.
Hollunderbüsche sacht am Weg verwehn;
Ein Haus zerflimmert wunderlich und vag.

In Goldnem schwebt ein Duft von Thymian,
Auf einem Stein steht eine heitere Zahl.
Auf einer Wiese spielen Kinder Ball,
Dann hebt ein Baum vor dir zu kreisen an.

Du träumst: die Schwester kämmt ihr blondes Haar,
Auch schreibt ein ferner Freund dir einen Brief.
Ein Schober flieht durchs Grau vergilbt und schief
Und manchmal schwebst du leicht und wunderbar.

2

Die Zeit verrinnt. O süßer Helios!
O Bild im Krötentümpel süß und klar;
Im Sand versinkt ein Eden wunderbar.
Goldammern wiegt ein Busch in seinem Schoß.

Ein Bruder stirbt dir in verwunschnem Land
Und stählern schaun dich deine Augen an.
In Goldnem dort ein Duft von Thymian.
Ein Knabe legt am Weiler einen Brand.

Die Liebenden in Faltern neu erglühn
Und schaukeln heiter hin um Stein und Zahl.
Aufflattern Krähen um ein ekles Mahl
Und deine Stirne tost durchs sanfte Grün.

Im Dornenstrauch verendet weich ein Wild.
Nachgleitet dir ein heller Kindertag,

THE STROLL

1

Music hums in the grove of afternoon.
In the wheat stern scarecrows whirl.
Elder bushes blow over softly along the path;
A house glimmers to pieces, strange and vague.

A scent of thyme hovers in the gold,
A bright number stands on a stone.
In a meadow children are playing ball,
Then a tree begins to lift and spin before you.

You dream: the sister combs her blonde hair,
And a faraway friend writes a letter to you.
A hay-rick flees through gray, yellowed and skewed
And sometimes you float, light and wonderful.

2

Time trickles away. O sweet Helios!
O image in the toad-pool, sweet and clear;
Wonderfully an Eden sinks into the sand.
A bush rocks yellowhammers in its lap.

A brother of yours dies in an enchanted land
And your eyes are staring at you like steel.
In the gold there a scent of thyme.
A boy sets a fire near the hamlet.

The lovers among butterflies glow again
And swing happily round stone and number.
Crows flutter up around a vile meal
And your forehead rages through the soft green.

In the thicket of thorns a deer softly dies.
A bright day of childhood glides after you,

Der graue Wind, der flatterhaft und vag.
Verfallne Düfte durch die Dämmerung spült.

3

Ein altes Wiegenlied macht dich sehr bang.
Am Wegrand fromm ein Weib ihr Kindlein stillt.
Traumwandelnd hörst du wie ihr Bronnen quillt.
Aus Apfelzweigen fällt ein Weiheklang.

Und Brot und Wein sind süß von harten Mühn.
Nach Früchten tastet silbern deine Hand.
Die tote Rahel geht durchs Ackerland.
Mit friedlicher Geberde winkt das Grün.

Gesegnet auch blüht armer Mägde Schoß,
Die träumend dort am alten Brunnen stehn.
Einsame froh auf stillen Pfaden gehn
Mit Gottes Kreaturen sündelos.

The gray wind, fickle and vague.
Flushes the dusk with decayed scents.

3

An ancient lullaby fills you with dread.
By the path a woman piously suckles her child.
Sleepwalking you hear her fountain swell.
A blessed sound falls from apple branches.

And bread and wine are sweetened by hard work.
Silvery your hand gropes for fruit.
Dead Rachel wanders through the farmland.
The green beckons with a peaceful gesture.

Blessed too the flowering wombs of poor maids,
Who stand there dreaming by the ancient well.
Merrily the lonely ones on silent paths
Walk sinless with God's creatures.

DE PROFUNDIS

Es ist ein Stoppelfeld, in das ein schwarzer Regen fällt.
Es ist ein brauner Baum, der einsam dasteht.
Es ist ein Zischelwind, der leere Hütten umkreist.
Wie traurig dieser Abend.

Am Weiler vorbei
Sammelt die sanfte Waise noch spärliche Ähren ein.
Ihre Augen weiden rund und goldig in der Dämmerung
Und ihr Schoß harrt des himmlischen Bräutigams.

Bei der Heimkehr
Fanden die Hirten den süßen Leib
Verwest im Dornenbusch.

Ein Schatten bin ich ferne finsteren Dörfern.
Gottes Schweigen
Trank ich aus dem Brunnen des Hains.

Auf meine Stirne tritt kaltes Metall
Spinnen suchen mein Herz.
Es ist ein Licht, das in meinem Mund erlöscht.

Nachts fand ich mich auf einer Heide,
Starrend von Unrat und Staub der Sterne.
Im Haselgebüsch
Klangen wieder kristallne Engel.

DE PROFUNDIS

It is a stubble field on which a black rain falls.
It is a brown tree that stands alone.
It is a hissing wind that circles empty shacks.
How sad this evening.

Beyond the hamlet
The gentle orphan still gathers sparse corn.
Her eyes graze round and golden in the dusk
And her womb awaits the heavenly bridegroom.

On their return
The shepherds found the sweet body
Putrid in the thorn bush.

I am a shadow far from sinister villages.
God's silence
I drank from the grove's well.

Cold metal steps on my forehead
Spiders search my heart.
It is a light that dies in my mouth.

At night I found myself on a heath,
Stiff with filth and the dust of stars.
In the hazel bush
Crystal angels chime once more.

TROMPETEN

Unter verschnittenen Weiden, wo braune Kinder spielen
Und Blätter treiben, tönen Trompeten. Ein Kirchhofsschauer.
Fahnen von Scharlach stürzen durch des Ahorns Trauer,
Reiter entlang an Roggenfeldern, leere Mühlen.

Oder Hirten singen nachts und Hirsche treten
In den Kreis ihrer Feuer, des Hains uralte Trauer,
Tanzende heben sich von einer schwarzen Mauer;
Fahnen von Scharlach, Lachen, Wahnsinn, Trompeten.

TRUMPETS

Beneath mutilated willows, where brown children play
And leaves drift, trumpets blare. A graveyard shudder.
Scarlet banners plunge through the maple's grief,
Horsemen along fields of rye, empty mills.

Or shepherds sing at night and stags enter
Into the circle of their fires, the grove's ancient sorrow,
Dancers rise from a black wall;
Scarlet banners, laughter, madness, trumpets.

DÄMMERUNG

In Hof, verhext von milchigem Dämmerschein,
Durch Herbstgebräuntes weiche Kranke gleiten.
Ihr wächsern-runder Blick sinnt goldner Zeiten,
Erfüllt von Träumerei und Ruh und Wein.

Ihr Siechentum schließt geisterhaft sich ein.
Die Sterne weiße Traurigkeit verbreiten.
Im Grau, erfüllt von Täuschung und Geläuten,
Sieh, wie die Schrecklichen sich wirr zerstreuen.

Formlose Spottgestalten huschen, kauern
Und flattern sie auf schwarz-gekreuzten Pfaden.
O! trauervolle Schatten an den Mauern.

Die andern fliehn durch dunkelnde Arkaden;
Und nächtens stürzen sie aus roten Schauern
Des Sternenwinds, gleich rasenden Mänaden.

TWILIGHT

In the courtyard, bewitched by twilight's milky glow,
Soft invalids glide through things autumn-browned.
Their waxen-round gaze ponders golden times,
Filled with reverie and peace and wine.

Their wasting disease shuts itself in like a ghost.
The stars are spreading white melancholy.
In the gray, filled with illusion and ringing bells,
See how the damned scatter in mad haste.

Formless objects of ridicule flit, cower
And flutter upon black-crossed paths.
O! mournful shadows on the walls.

The others flee through darkening arcades;
And at night they plunge from red shudders
Of the star wind, like frantic maenads.

HEITERER FRÜHLING

2. Fassung

1

Am Bach, der durch das gelbe Brachfeld fließt,
Zieht noch das dürre Rohr vom vorigen Jahr.
Durchs Graue gleiten Klänge wunderbar,
Vorüberweht ein Hauch von warmem Mist.

An Weiden baumeln Kätzchen sacht im Wind,
Sein traurig Lied singt träumend ein Soldat.
Ein Wiesenstreifen saust verweht und matt,
Ein Kind steht in Konturen weich und lind.

Die Birken dort, der schwarze Dornenstrauch,
Auch fliehn im Rauch Gestalten aufgelöst.
Hell Grünes blüht und anderes verwest
Und Kröten schliefen durch den jungen Lauch.

2

Dich lieb ich treu du derbe Wäscherin.
Noch trägt die Flut des Himmels goldene Last.
Ein Fischlein blitzt vorüber und verblaßt;
Ein wächsern Antlitz fließt durch Erlen hin.

In Gärten sinken Glocken lang und leis
Ein kleiner Vogel trällert wie verrückt.
Das sanfte Korn schwillt leise und verzückt
Und Bienen sammeln noch mit ernstem Fleiß.

Komm Liebe nun zum müden Arbeitsmann!
In seine Hütte fällt ein lauer Strahl.
Der Wald strömt durch den Abend herb und fahl
Und Knospen knistern heiter dann und wann.

BRIGHT SPRING

2nd Version

1

By the brook that runs through the yellow fallow field,
Last year's withered reed still rustles.
Sounds glide wonderfully through the gray,
A breath of warm manure drifts by.

On willows catkins dangle gently in the wind,
A dreaming soldier sings his mournful song.
A strip of meadow soughs windswept and faint,
A child stands in silhouette soft and tender.

The birches there, the black briers,
And dissolved figures also flee in smoke.
Things bright-green bloom and others rot
And toads slept through the young leek.

2

You I love truly, my rough washerwoman.
The flood still carries heaven's golden load.
A little fish flashes past and fades;
A waxen face flows through alders.

In gardens bells sink long and low,
A little bird trills like crazy.
The gentle wheat swells softly and raptly
And bees still gather with earnest diligence.

Come, love, to the tired workingman!
Into his cottage falls a tepid beam of light.
The forest streams through evening harsh and pale
And now and then buds crackle gaily.

3

Wie scheint doch alles Werdende so krank!
Ein Fieberhauch um einen Weiler kreist;
Doch aus Gezweigen winkt ein sanfter Geist
Und öffnet das Gemüte weit und bang.

Ein blühender Erguß verrinnt sehr sacht
Und Ungebornes pflegt der eignen Ruh.
Die Liebenden blühn ihren Sternen zu
Und süßer fließt ihr Odem durch die Nacht.

So schmerzlich gut und wahrhaft ist, was lebt;
Und leise rührt dich an ein alter Stein:
Wahrlich! Ich werde immer bei euch sein.
O Mund! der durch die Silberweide bebt.

3

But how all this growing seems so sick!
A breath of fever circles a hamlet;
Yet from branches a gentle spirit beckons
And opens the soul fearful and wide.

A blossoming outpour leaks away very gently
And things unborn rest in their own peace.
Lovers bloom toward their stars
And their breath flows sweeter through the night.

So painfully good and true is all that lives;
And softly an ancient stone touches you:
Truly! I will always be with you.
O mouth! that quakes through the white willow.

VORSTADT IM FÖHN

Am Abend liegt die Stätte öd und braun,
Die Luft von gräulichem Gestank durchzogen.
Das Donnern eines Zugs vom Brückenbogen –
Und Spatzen flattern über Busch und Zaun.

Geduckte Hütten, Pfade wirr verstreut,
In Gärten Durcheinander und Bewegung,
Bisweilen schwillt Geheul aus dumpfer Regung,
In einer Kinderschar fliegt rot ein Kleid.

Am Kehricht pfeift verliebt ein Rattenchor.
In Körben tragen Frauen Eingeweide,
Ein ekelhafter Zug voll Schmutz und Räude,
Kommen sie aus der Dämmerung hervor.

Und ein Kanal speit plötzlich feistes Blut
Vom Schlachthaus in den stillen Fluß hinunter.
Die Föhne färben karge Stauden bunter
Und langsam kriecht die Röte durch die Flut.

Ein Flüstern, das in trübem Schlaf ertrinkt.
Gebilde gaukeln auf aus Wassergräben,
Vielleicht Erinnerung an ein früheres Leben,
Die mit den warmen Winden steigt und sinkt.

Aus Wolken tauchen schimmernde Alleen,
Erfüllt von schönen Wägen, kühnen Reitern.
Dann sieht man auch ein Schiff auf Klippen scheitern
Und manchmal rosenfarbene Moscheen.

SUBURB IN FÖHN

At evening the place lies desolate and brown,
A gray stench permeates the air.
The roar of a train from the arched bridge—
And sparrows flutter over bush and fence.

Humble shacks, paths scattered in chaos,
In the gardens disorder and movement,
Sometimes howls swell from muffled motion,
A red dress flies through a crowd of children.

By the rubbish a chorus of rats' spoony whistles.
Women carry entrails in baskets,
A vile procession full of filth and mange,
They emerge from the twilight.

And a canal suddenly spews fat and blood
From the slaughterhouse down into the calm river.
Föhn winds color the sparse shrubs brighter
And the redness creeps slowly through the torrent.

A whispering that drowns in troubled sleep.
Shapes leap up from water drains,
Perhaps the memory of an earlier life,
Which rises and falls with warm winds.

Gleaming avenues loom from the clouds,
Filled with beautiful chariots, bold riders.
Then you also see a wrecked ship along the cliffs
And sometimes rose-colored mosques.

DIE RATTEN

In Hof scheint weiß der herbstliche Mond.
Vom Dachrand fallen phantastische Schatten.
Ein Schweigen in leeren Fenstern wohnt;
Da tauchen leise herauf die Ratten

Und huschen pfeifend hier und dort
Und ein gräulicher Dunsthauch wittert
Ihnen nach aus dem Abort,
Den geisterhaft der Mondschein durchzittert

Und sie keifen vor Gier wie toll
Und erfüllen Haus und Scheunen,
Die von Korn und Früchten voll.
Eisige Winde im Dunkel greinen.

THE RATS

The fall moon shines white in the yard.
Fantastic shadows plunge off the roof ends.
A silence dwells in empty windows;
Then the rats come up softly

And scurry this way, that way, like flutes
And a dreadful stench from the privy
Stinks after them,
Through which the ghostly moonlight shudders.

And they shriek eagerly as if mad
And crowd house and stores
That are filled with grain and fruit.
Icy winds moan in the dark.

TRÜBSINN

1. Fassung

Weltunglück geistert durch den Nachmittag.
Baraken fliehn durch Gärtchen braun und wüst.
Lichtschnuppen gaukeln um verbrannten Mist,
Zwei Schläfer schwanken heimwärts, grau und vag.

Auf der verdorrten Wiese läuft ein Kind
Und spielt mit seinen Augen schwarz und glatt.
Das Gold tropft von den Büschen trüb und matt.
Ein alter Mann dreht traurig sich im Wind.

Am Abend wieder über meinem Haupt
Saturn lenkt stumm ein elendes Geschick.
Ein Baum, ein Hund tritt hinter sich zurück
Und schwarz schwankt Gottes Himmel und entlaubt.

Ein Fischlein gleitet schnell hinab den Bach;
Und leise rührt des toten Freundes Hand
Und glättet liebend Stirne und Gewand.
Ein Licht ruft Schatten in den Zimmern wach.

DEPRESSION

World-misery ghosts through the afternoon.
Sheds flee through little gardens brown and wasted.
Shooting lights sway around scorched dung,
Two sleepers stagger homeward, gray and vague.

A child walks on the parched meadow
And plays with her eyes black and smooth.
Gold drips from the bushes dull and flat.
An old man spins sadly in the wind.

In the evening again over my head
Mute Saturn guides a wretched fate.
A tree, a dog steps back behind itself
And God's heaven falters black and sheds its leaves.

A small fish glides swiftly down the brook;
And gently the dead friend's hand moves
And lovingly smooths forehead and robe.
A light rouses shadows in the rooms.

IN DEN NACHMITTAG GEFLÜSTERT

Sonne, herbstlich dünn und zag,
Und das Obst fällt von den Bäumen.
Stille wohnt in blauen Räumen
Einen langen Nachmittag.

Sterbeklänge von Metall;
Und ein weißes Tier bricht nieder.
Brauner Mädchen rauhe Lieder
Sind verweht im Blätterfall.

Stirne Gottes Farben träumt,
Spürt des Wahnsinns sanfte Flügel.
Schatten drehen sich am Hügel
Von Verwesung schwarz umsäumt.

Dämmerung voll Ruh und Wein;
Traurige Guitarren rinnen.
Und zur milden Lampe drinnen
Kehrst du wie im Traume ein.

WHISPERED INTO THE AFTERNOON

Sun, thin like autumn and shy,
And fruit drops from the trees.
Silence dwells in blue chambers
A long afternoon.

Dying sounds of metal;
And a white beast collapses.
Brown girls' rough songs
Scattered in falling leaves.

God's forehead dreams colors,
Feels the gentle wings of madness.
Shadows are spinning upon the hill
Fringed black with decay.

Twilight full of rest and wine;
Mournful guitars are flowing.
And to the mild lamp inside
You come as in a dream.

PSALM

2. Fassung

Karl Kraus zugeeignet

Es ist ein Licht, das der Wind ausgelöscht hat.
Es ist ein Heidekrug, den am Nachmittag ein Betrunkener verläßt.
Es ist ein Weinberg, verbrannt und Schwarz mit Löchern voll
    Spinnen.
Es ist ein Raum, den sie mit Milch getüncht haben.
Der Wahnsinnige ist gestorben. Es ist eine Insel der Südsee,
Den Sonnengott zu empfangen. Man rührt die Trommeln.
Die Männer führen kriegerische Tänze auf.
Die Frauen wiegen die Hüften in Schlinggewächsen und
    Feuerblumen,
Wenn das Meer singt. O unser verlorenes Paradies.

Die Nymphen haben die goldenen Wälder verlassen.
Man begräbt den Fremden. Dann hebt ein Flimmerregen an.
Der Sohn des Pan erscheint in Gestalt eines Erdarbeiters,
Der den Mittag am glühenden Asphalt verschläft.
Es sind kleine Mädchen in einem Hof in Kleidchen voll
    herzzerreißender Armut!
Es sind Zimmer, erfüllt von Akkorden und Sonaten.
Es sind Schatten, die sich vor einem erblindeten Spiegel
    umarmen.
An den Fenstern des Spitals wärmen sich Genesende.
Ein weißer Dampfer am Kanal trägt blutige Seuchen herauf.

Die fremde Schwester erscheint wieder in jemands bösen
    Träumen.
Ruhend im Haselgebüsch spielt sie mit seinen Sternen.
Der Student, vielleicht ein Doppelgänger, schaut ihr lange vom
    Fenster nach.
Hinter ihm steht sein toter Bruder, oder er geht die alte
    Wendeltreppe herab.
Im Dunkel brauner Kastanien verblaßt die Gestalt des jungen
    Novizen.

PSALM

2nd Version

Dedicated to Karl Kraus

It is a light the wind has extinguished.
It is a tavern a drunkard leaves in the afternoon.
It is a vineyard, burnt and black with holes full of spiders.
It is a room they have whitewashed with milk.
The madman has died. It is an island in the South Seas
There to receive the sun god. They are beating the drums.
The men perform warlike dances.
The women sway their hips in lianas and fiery flowers,
When the sea sings. O our lost paradise.

The nymphs have abandoned the golden forests.
The stranger is buried. Then a glimmering rain begins to fall.
The son of Pan appears in the guise of an excavator,
Who sleeps through noon by the smoldering asphalt.
There are young girls in a courtyard in little dresses full of
    heartbreaking poverty!
There are rooms abuzz with chords and sonatas.
There are shadows embracing before a blinded mirror.
Convalescents warm themselves by the windows of the hospital.
A white steamer on the canal carries bloody plagues upstream.

The strange sister appears again in someone's evil dreams.
Resting in the hazel bush she plays with his stars.
The student, perhaps a doppelgänger, watches long after her
    from the window.
His dead brother stands behind him, or he descends the old
    spiral staircase.
In the dark of brown chestnuts the young novice's figure fades.
The garden is inside the evening. Bats flutter about in the cloister.
The caretaker's children stop their play and search for the gold
    of heaven.
A quartet's final chords. The small blind girl runs trembling
    through the avenue,

Der Garten ist im Abend. Im Kreuzgang flattern die
Fledermäuse umher.
Die Kinder des Hausmeisters hören zu spielen auf und suchen
das Gold des Himmels.
Endakkorde eines Quartetts. Die kleine Blinde läuft zitternd
durch die Allee,
Und später tastet ihr Schatten an kalten Mauern hin, umgeben
von
Märchen und heiligen Legenden.

Es ist ein leeres Boot, das am Abend den schwarzen Kanal
heruntertreibt.
In der Düsternis des alten Asyls verfallen menschliche Ruinen.
Die toten Waisen liegen an der Gartenmauer.
Aus grauen Zimmern treten Engel mit kotgefleckten Flügeln.
Würmer tropfen von ihren vergilbten Lidern.
Der Platz vor der Kirche ist finster und schweigsam, wie in den
Tagen der Kindheit.
Auf silbernen Sohlen gleiten frühere Leben vorbei
Und die Schatten der Verdammten steigen zu den seufzenden
Wassern nieder.
In seinem Grab spielt der weiße Magier mit seinen Schlangen.
Schweigsam über der Schädelstätte öffnen sich Gottes goldene
Augen.

And later her shadow gropes along cold walls, surrounded by
    fairy
Tales and holy legends.

It is an empty boat that drifts down the black canal in the
    evening.
Human ruins decay in the gloom of the old asylum.
The dead orphans lie by the garden wall.
Angels with feces-spotted wings emerge from gray rooms.
Worms drip from their yellowed eyelids.
The church square is dark and silent as in the days of
    childhood.
Earlier lives glide by on silvery soles
And the shadows of the damned descend to the sighing waters.
In his grave the white magician plays with his snakes.
Above Mount Calvary God's golden eyes open in silence.

ROSENKRANZLIEDER

AN DIE SCHWESTER

Wo du gehst wird Herbst und Abend,
Blaues Wild, das unter Bäumen tönt,
Einsamer Weiher am Abend.

Leise der Flug der Vögel tönt,
Die Schwermut über deinen Augenbogen.
Dein schmales Lächeln tönt.

Gott hat deine Lider verbogen.
Sterne suchen nachts, Karfreitagskind,
Deinen Stirnenbogen.

HYMNS FOR A ROSARY

TO THE SISTER

Wherever you go, you bring autumn and evening,
Sounds of blue deer beneath the trees,
The lonely evening pond.

Soft sounds of birds in flight,
The sadness above your eyelids.
Sounds of your narrow smile.

God has bent your eyelids.
At night stars seek, Good Friday's child,
The arch of your brow.

NÄHE DES TODES

2. Fassung

O der Abend, der in die finsteren Dörfer der Kindheit geht.
Der Weiher unter den Weiden
Füllt sich mit den verpesteten Seufzern der Schwermut.

O der Wald, der leise die braunen Augen senkt,
Da aus des Einsamen knöchernen Händen
Der Purpur seiner verzückten Tage hinsinkt.

O die Nähe des Todes. Laß uns beten.
In dieser Nacht lösen auf lauen Kissen
Vergilbt von Weihrauch sich der Liebenden schmächtige
    Glieder.

NEARNESS OF DEATH

2nd Version

O the evening that enters the dark villages of childhood.
The pond beneath the willows
Fills itself with the poisoned sighs of melancholy.

O the forest that softly lowers its brown eyes,
When from the lonely one's bony hands
The crimson of his days of ecstasy fades away.

O the nearness of death. Let us pray.
In this night on warm pillows yellowed by incense
The delicate limbs of lovers part.

AMEN

Verwestes gleitend durch die morsche Stube;
Schatten an gelben Tapeten; in dunklen Spiegeln wölbt
Sich unserer Hände elfenbeinerne Traurigkeit.

Braune Perlen rinnen durch die erstorbenen Finger.
In der Stille
Tun sich eines Engels blaue Mohnaugen auf.

Blau ist auch der Abend;
Die Stunde unseres Absterbens, Azraels Schatten,
Der ein braunes Gärtchen verdunkelt.

AMEN

A thing decayed glides through the rotten chamber;
Shadows on yellow wallpaper; in dark mirrors
The ivory sorrow of our hands forms an arch.

Brown pearls trickle through dead fingers.
In the silence
An angel's blue poppy-eyes open.

The evening too is blue;
The hour of our dying, Azrael's shadow
That darkens a small brown garden.

VERFALL

Am Abend, wenn die Glocken Frieden läuten,
Folg ich der Vögel wundervollen Flügen,
Die lang geschart, gleich frommen Pilgerzügen,
Entschwinden in den herbstlich klaren Weiten.

Hinwandeln durch den dämmervollen Garten
Träum ich nach ihren helleren Geschicken
Und fühl der Stunden Weiser kaum mehr rücken.
So folg ich über Wolken ihren Fahrten.

Da macht ein Hauch mich von Verfall erzittern.
Die Amsel klagt in den entlaubten Zweigen.
Es schwankt der rote Wein an rostigen Gittern,

Indes wie blasser Kinder Todesreigen
Um dunkle Brunnenränder, die verwittern,
Im Wind sich fröstelnd blaue Astern neigen.

DECAY

In the evening, when the bells ring peace,
I follow the miraculous flights of birds
That in long flocks, like lines of pious pilgrims,
Vanish in clear autumnal skies.

Strolling through the dusky garden
I dream after their brighter fates
And barely feel the hour hands move.
Thus above clouds I follow their journeys.

Then a whiff of decay makes me tremble.
The blackbird laments in the leafless branches.
The red wine sways on rusty trellises,

While like the pale children's death-dance
Around dark rims of weathered fountains,
Blue asters bow and shiver in the wind.

IN DER HEIMAT

Resedenduft durchs kranke Fenster irrt;
Ein alter Platz, Kastanien schwarz und wüst.
Das Dach durchbricht ein goldener Strahl und fließt
Auf die Geschwister traumhaft und verwirrt.

Im Spülicht treibt Verfallnes, leise girrt
Der Föhn im braunen Gärtchen; sehr still genießt
Ihr Gold die Sonnenblume und zerfließt.
Durch blaue Luft der Ruf der Wache klirrt.

Resedenduft. Die Mauern dämmern kahl.
Der Schwester Schlaf ist schwer. Der Nachtwind wühlt
In ihrem Haar, das mondner Glanz umspült.

Der Katze Schatten gleitet blau und schmal
Vom morschen Dach, das nahes Unheil säumt,
Die Kerzenflamme, die sich purpurn bäumt.

IN THE HOMELAND

Scent of mignonettes strays through the sick window;
An old square, chestnuts black and wasted.
A golden ray breaks through the roof and flows
Onto the siblings, dreamlike and confused.

Decayed things float in the slop, the föhn wind
Coos softly in the small brown garden; very quietly
The sunflower enjoys its gold and melts away.
The watchman's cry rings through blue air.

Scent of mignonettes. Bare walls grow dark.
The sister's sleep is heavy. The night wind delves
Through her hair bathed by lunar glow.

The cat's shadow glides blue and slender
From the rotten roof hemmed by coming misery,
The crimson rearing of a candle's flame.

EIN HERBSTABEND

An Karl Röck

Das braune Dorf. Ein Dunkles zeigt im Schreiten
Sich oft an Mauern, die im Herbste stehn,
Gestalten: Mann wie Weib, Verstorbene gehn
In kühlen Stuben jener Bett bereiten.

Hier spielen Knaben. Schwere Schatten breiten
Sich über braune Jauche. Mägde gehn
Durch feuchte Bläue und bisweilen sehn
Aus Augen sie, erfüllt von Nachtgeläuten.

Für Einsames ist eine Schenke da;
Das säumt geduldig unter dunklen Bogen,
Von goldenem Tabaksgewölk umzogen.

Doch immer ist das Eigne schwarz und nah.
Der Trunkne sinnt im Schatten alter Bogen
Den wilden Vögeln nach, die ferngezogen.

AN AUTUMN EVENING

To Karl Röck

The brown village. Something dark often appears
Striding along walls that stand in autumn,
Figures: men and women, the deceased walk
In cool chambers to prepare their beds.

Here boys play. Heavy shadows spread
Over brown manure. Maidens walk
Through moist blueness and at times gaze
From eyes filled with nocturnal bells.

There's a tavern here for the lonely things;
It tarries patiently beneath dark arches,
Encircled by clouds of golden tobacco.

But always the self is black and near.
In the shadow of ancient arches the drunkard
Broods upon the migration of wild birds.

MENSCHLICHES ELEND

«Menschliche Trauer» *2. Fassung*

Die Uhr, die vor der Sonne fünfe schlägt –
Einsame Menschen packt ein dunkles Grausen,
Im Abendgarten kahle Bäume sausen.
Des Toten Antlitz sich am Fenster regt.

Vielleicht, daß diese Stunde stille steht.
Vor trüben Augen blaue Bilder gaukeln
Im Takt der Schiffe, die am Flusse schaukeln.
Am Kai ein Schwesternzug vorüberweht.

Im Hasel spielen Mädchen blaß und blind,
Wie Liebende, die sich im Schlaf umschlingen.
Vielleicht, daß um ein Aas dort Fliegen singen,
Vielleicht auch weint im Mutterschoß ein Kind.

Aus Händen sinken Astern blau und rot,
Des Jünglings Mund entgleitet fremd und weise;
Und Lider flattern angstverwirrt und leise;
Durch Fieberschwärze weht ein Duft von Brot.

Es scheint, man hört auch gräßliches Geschrei;
Gebeine durch verfallne Mauern schimmern.
Ein böses Herz lacht laut in schönen Zimmern;
An einem Träumer läuft ein Hund vorbei.

Ein leerer Sarg im Dunkel sich verliert.
Dem Mörder will ein Raum sich bleich erhellen,
Indes Laternen nachts im Sturm zerschellen.
Des Edlen weiße Schläfe Lorbeer ziert.

HUMAN MISERY

"Human Grief" *2nd Version*

The clock that strikes five before the sun—
Lonely people are seized by a dark terror,
Bare trees sough in the evening garden.
The dead man's face moves by the window.

Perhaps this hour has stopped.
Before glazed eyes blue images juggle
To the rhythm of ships that rock on the river.
A flight of nuns blows by on the landing.

Pale and blind girls play in the hazel bush,
Like lovers who embrace each other in sleep.
Perhaps there flies are singing over a carcass,
Perhaps too a child is weeping in her mother's lap.

From hands asters sink blue and red,
The boy's mouth slips away strange and wise;
And eyelids dazed by fear flutter softly;
The scent of bread wafts through fever's blackness.

It seems you can also hear terrible screaming;
Old bones shimmer through crumbled walls.
An evil heart laughs out loud in beautiful rooms;
A dog runs past a dreaming man.

An empty coffin loses itself in the dark.
A room wants to brighten palely for the murderer,
While lanterns shatter in the storm by night.
Laurels grace the noble one's white temples.

IM DORF

1

Aus braunen Mauern tritt ein Dorf, ein Feld.
Ein Hirt verwest auf einem alten Stein.
Der Saum des Walds schließt blaue Tiere ein,
Das sanfte Laub, das in die Stille fällt.

Der Bauern braune Stirnen. Lange tönt
Die Abendglocke; schön ist frommer Brauch,
Des Heilands schwarzes Haupt im Dornenstrauch,
Die kühle Stube, die der Tod versöhnt.

Wie bleich die Mütter sind. Die Bläue sinkt
Auf Glas und Truh, die stolz ihr Sinn bewahrt;
Auch neigt ein weißes Haupt sich hochbejahrt
Aufs Enkelkind, das Milch und Sterne trinkt.

2

Der Arme, der im Geiste einsam starb,
Steigt wächsern über einen alten Pfad.
Die Apfelbäume sinken kahl und stad
Ins Farbige ihrer Frucht, die schwarz verdarb.

Noch immer wölbt das Dach aus dürrem Stroh
Sich übern Schlaf der Kühe. Die blinde Magd
Erscheint in Hof; ein blaues Wasser klagt;
Ein Pferdeschädel starrt vom morschen Tor.

Der Idiot spricht dunklen Sinns ein Wort
Der Liebe, das im schwarzen Busch verhallt,
Wo jene steht in schmaler Traumgestalt.
Der Abend tönt in feuchter Bläue fort.

IN THE VILLAGE

1

From brown walls emerges a village, a field.
A shepherd decays on an ancient stone.
The forest's edge traps blue animals,
The soft leaves that fall into silence.

The peasants' brown foreheads. Long rings
The evening bell; pious custom is beautiful,
The Savior's black head wreathed in thorns,
The cool chamber which death reconciles.

How pale the mothers are. The blueness sinks
Onto glass and chest that keep them in mind;
Also an age-old white head bends over
The grandchild, who drinks milk and stars.

2

The poor man who died lonely in spirit
Steps waxen over an ancient path.
The apple trees sink bare and calm
Into the colors of their fruit spoiled black.

The roof of dried straw still arches
Above the sleep of cows. The blind maid
Appears in the courtyard; a blue water grieves.
A horse's skull stares from the rotten gate.

With a darkened mind the idiot speaks a word
Of love that fades away in the black bush,
Where she stands in her slender dream-shape.
Evening continues to sound in damp blue.

3

Ans Fenster schlagen Äste föhnentlaubt.
Im Schoß der Bäurin wächst ein wildes Weh.
Durch ihre Arme rieselt schwarzer Schnee;
Goldäugige Eulen flattern um ihr Haupt.

Die Mauern starren kahl und grauverdreckt
Ins kühle Dunkel. Im Fieberbette friert
Der schwangere Leib, den frech der Mond bestiert.
Vor ihrer Kammer ist ein Hund verreckt.

Drei Männer treten finster durch das Tor
Mit Sensen, die im Feld zerbrochen sind.
Durchs Fenster klirrt der rote Abendwind;
Ein schwarzer Engel tritt daraus hervor.

3

Branches bared by the föhn wind beat against the window.
A wild pain grows in the farmwife's womb.
Black snow trickles through her arms;
Golden-eyed owls flutter around her head.

The walls stare bare and gray with dirt
Into cool darkness. The pregnant body chills
In the fever bed, stared at by a brash moon.
A dog has died in front of her chamber.

Three men come in darkly through the gate
With scythes shattered in the field.
The red evening wind rattles through the window;
A black angel emerges from it.

ABENDLIED

Am Abend, wenn wir auf dunklen Pfaden gehn,
Erscheinen unsere bleichen Gestalten vor uns.

Wenn uns dürstet,
Trinken wir die weißen Wasser des Teichs,
Die Süße unserer traurigen Kindheit.

Erstorbene ruhen wir unterm Hollundergebüsch,
Schaun den grauen Möven zu.

Frühlingsgewölke steigen über die finstere Stadt,
Die der Mönche edlere Zeiten schweigt.

Da ich deine schmalen Hände nahm
Schlugst du leise die runden Augen auf,
Dieses ist lange her.

Doch wenn dunkler Wohllaut die Seele heimsucht,
Erscheinst du Weiße in des Freundes herbstlicher Landschaft.

EVENING SONG

At evening, when we walk down dark paths,
Our pale figures appear before us.

When we thirst,
We drink the white waters of the pond,
The sweetness of our wretched childhood.

Dead, we rest beneath the elder bushes,
Watching the gray gulls.

Spring clouds rise over the dark town
That veils the nobler ages of monks.

When I took your slender hands
You opened your round eyes softly,
That was long ago.

But when a dark melody haunts the soul,
You emerge white in the friend's autumnal landscape.

DREI BLICKE IN EINEN OPAL

An Erhard Buschbeck

1

Blick in Opal: ein Dorf umkränzt von dürrem Wein,
Der Stille grauer Wolken, gelber Felsenhügel
Und abendlicher Quellen Kühle: Zwillingsspiegel
Umrahmt von Schatten und von schleimigem Gestein.

Des Herbstes Weg und Kreuze gehn in Abend ein,
Singende Pilger und die blutbefleckten Linnen.
Des Einsamen Gestalt kehrt also sich nach innen
Und geht, ein bleicher Engel, durch den leeren Hain.

Aus Schwarzem bläst der Föhn. Mit Satyrn im Verein
Sind schlanke Weiblein; Mönche der Wollust bleiche Priester,
Ihr Wahnsinn schmückt mit Lilien sich schön und düster
Und hebt die Hände auf zu Gottes goldenem Schrein.

2

Der ihn befeuchtet, rosig hängt ein Tropfen Tau
Im Rosmarin: hinfließt ein Hauch von Grabgerüchen,
Spitälern, wirr erfüllt von Fieberschrein und Flüchen.
Gebein steigt aus dem Erbbegräbnis morsch und grau.

In blauem Schleim und Schleiern tanzt des Greisen Frau,
Das schmutzstarrende Haar erfüllt von schwarzen Tränen,
Die Knaben träumen wirr in dürren Weidensträhnen
Und ihre Stirnen sind von Aussatz kahl und rauh.

Durchs Bogenfenster sinkt ein Abend lind und lau.
Ein Heiliger tritt aus seinen schwarzen Wundenmalen.
Die Purpurschnecken kriechen aus zerbrochenen Schalen
Und speien Blut in Dorngewinde starr und grau.

THREE GLIMPSES INTO AN OPAL

To Erhard Buschbeck

1

Glimpse into opal: a village wreathed by seared vines,
The gray clouds of silence, yellow hill of rocks
And chill of an evening spring: twin mirrors
Framed by shadows and by slimy stones.

Autumn's path and crosses enter evening,
Singing pilgrims and the blood-spattered linens.
So the lonely one's figure turns inward
And walks, a pale angel, through the empty grove.

The föhn wind blows out of something black. Little slender
Women and satyrs in unison; monks, pale priests of lust,
Their madness adorns itself with lilies dark and lovely
And lifts its hands to God's golden shrine.

2

Moistening it, a pink drop of dew hangs
In the rosemary: a breath of graveyard odors fades away,
Of hospitals, filled with crazed fever-screams and curses.
Bones climb from the family vault rotten and gray.

The old man's wife dances in blue slime and mists,
Her dirt-stiffened hair filled with black tears,
The boys' crazed dreams in the seared strands of willows
And leprosy has turned their foreheads bald and raw.

An evening sinks through the arched window mild and soft.
A saint emerges from his black stigmatic wounds.
Crimson murices crawl from broken shells
And spew blood in winding thorns stiff and gray.

3

Die Blinden streuen in eiternde Wunden Weiherauch.
Rotgoldene Gewänder; Fackeln; Psalmensingen;
Und Mädchen, die wie Gift den Leib des Herrn umschlingen.
Gestalten schreiten wächsernstarr durch Glut und Rauch.

Aussätziger mitternächtigen Tanz führt an ein Gauch
Dürrknöchern. Garten wunderlicher Abenteuer;
Verzerrtes; Blumenfratzen, Lachen; Ungeheuer
Und rollendes Gestirn im schwarzen Dornenstrauch.

O Armut, Bettelsuppe, Brot und süßer Lauch;
Des Lebens Träumerei in Hütten vor den Wäldern.
Grau härtet sich der Himmel über gelben Feldern
Und eine Abendglocke singt nach altem Brauch.

3

The blind spread incense in festering wounds.
Red-golden garments; torches; singing of psalms;
And girls who embrace the Lord's body like poison.
Figures walk stiff as wax through embers and smoke.

A dry-boned fool leads the lepers' dance
At midnight. Gardens of strange adventures;
Distorted things; grimacing flowers, laughter; monsters
And rolling constellations in the black briar.

O poverty, beggar's soup, bread and sweet leek;
Life's daydreams in shacks near the forests.
The sky hardens to gray over yellow fields
And following old custom an evening bell sings.

NACHTLIED

Des Unbewegten Odem. Ein Tiergesicht
Erstarrt vor Bläue, ihrer Heiligkeit.
Gewaltig ist das Schweigen im Stein;

Die Maske eines nächtlichen Vogels. Sanfter Dreiklang
Verklingt in einem. Elai! dein Antlitz
Beugt sich sprachlos über bläuliche Wasser.

O! ihr stillen Spiegel der Wahrheit.
An des Einsamen elfenbeinerner Schläfe
Erscheint der Abglanz gefallener Engel.

NOCTURNE

Breath of the unmoved. An animal face
Stiffens with blue, its holiness.
Monstrous is the silence inside stone;

The mask of a night bird. A silken triad
Fades to a single note. Elai! your face
Bends over blue waters speechless.

O! you silent mirrors of truth.
On one side of his elephant ivory brow
The lonely one reveals the glory of fallen angels.

HELIAN

In den einsamen Stunden des Geistes
Ist es schön, in der Sonne zu gehn
An den gelben Mauern des Sommers hin.
Leise klingen die Schritte im Gras; doch immer schläft
Der Sohn des Pan im grauen Marmor.

Abends auf der Terrasse betranken wir uns mit braunem Wein.
Rötlich glüht der Pfirsich im Laub;
Sanfte Sonate, frohes Lachen.

Schön ist die Stille der Nacht.
Auf dunklem Plan
Begegnen wir uns mit Hirten und weißen Sternen.

Wenn es Herbst geworden ist
Zeigt sich nüchterne Klarheit im Hain.
Besänftigte wandeln wir an roten Mauern hin
Und die runden Augen folgen dem Flug der Vögel.
Am Abend sinkt das weiße Wasser in Graburnen.

In kahlen Gezweigen feiert der Himmel.
In reinen Händen trägt der Landmann Brot und Wein
Und friedlich reifen die Früchte in sonniger Kammer.

O wie ernst ist das Antlitz der teueren Toten.
Doch die Seele erfreut gerechtes Anschaun.

Gewaltig ist das Schweigen des verwüsteten Gartens,
Da der junge Novize die Stirne mit braunem Laub bekränzt,
Sein Odem eisiges Gold trinkt.

Die Hände rühren das Alter bläulicher Wasser
Oder in kalter Nacht die weißen Wangen der Schwestern.

HELIAN

In the lonely hours of reverie
It is fine to walk in the sun
Along summer's yellow walls.
Softly footsteps ring in the grass; yet always
Pan's son sleeps in the gray marble.

At evening on the terrace we got drunk on bronze wine.
The peach glows red in the leaves;
Gentle sonata, gay laughter.

The silence of night is wonderful.
On a dark plain
We meet ourselves with shepherds and white stars.

When autumn has arrived
A sober clarity shows itself in the grove.
Satisfied we stroll along red walls
And our wide eyes follow the passage of birds.
In the evening the white water sinks in funeral urns.

The sky celebrates in bare branches.
In pure hands the peasant carries bread and wine
And fruit ripens peacefully in a sunlit pantry.

O how somber is the face of the cherished dead.
But the soul takes comfort with a righteous gaze.

Immense is the silence of the ruined garden,
Where the young novice crowns himself with brown leaves,
His breath drinks icy gold.

Hands stir the vintage of blue waters
Or in cold night the sisters' white cheeks.

Leise und harmonisch ist ein Gang an freundlichen Zimmern
  hin,
Wo Einsamkeit ist und das Rauschen des Ahorns,
Wo vielleicht noch die Drossel singt.

Schön ist der Mensch und erscheinend im Dunkel,
Wenn er staunend Arme und Beine bewegt
Und in purpurnen Höhlen stille die Augen rollen.

Zur Vesper verliert sich der Fremdling in schwarzer
  Novemberzerstörung,
Unter morschen Geäst, an Mauern voll Aussatz hin,
Wo vordem der heilige Bruder gegangen,
Versunken in das sanfte Saitenspiel seines Wahnsinns,

O wie einsam endet der Abendwind.
Ersterbend neigt sich das Haupt im Dunkel des Ölbaums.

Erschütternd ist der Untergang des Geschlechts.
In dieser Stunde füllen sich die Augen des Schauenden
Mit dem Gold seiner Sterne.

Am Abend versinkt ein Glockenspiel, das nicht mehr tönt,
Verfallen die schwarzen Mauern am Platz,
Ruft der tote Soldat zum Gebet.

Ein bleicher Engel
Tritt der Sohn ins leere Haus seiner Väter.

Die Schwestern sind ferne zu weißen Greisen gegangen.
Nachts fand sie der Schläfer unter den Säulen im Hausflur,
Zurückgekehrt von traurigen Pilgerschaften.

O wie starrt von Kot und Würmern ihr Haar,
Da er darein mit silbernen Füßen steht,
Und jene verstorben aus kahlen Zimmern treten.

Soft and melodic is a walk past cheerful rooms,
Where solitude dwells and the maple's rustle,
Where perhaps the thrush still sings.

Mankind is beautiful when seen in the dark,
When he stretches his arms and legs astonished,
And calm in their crimson caves eyes look all around.

At vespers the stranger loses himself in November's black ruin,
Beneath rotten branches, past walls filled with leprosy,
Where earlier the holy brother walked,
Drowned in the soft lyre-play of his madness,

O how lonely ends the evening wind.
The head nods away into the dark of the olive tree and dies.

Shocking is the decline of this generation.
In this hour the eyes of the witness
Fill with the gold of his stars.

No longer played, a glockenspiel goes down at night,
Black walls crumble on the square,
The dead soldier makes the call to prayer.

A pale angel
The son enters his fathers' empty house.

The sisters have gone to white old men faraway.
At night the sleeper found them beneath the pillars in the
      hallway,
Each returned from her tarnished pilgrimages.

O how their hair is stiff with feces and worms,
That in which he stands with silvery feet,
And those dead step from bare rooms.

O ihr Psalmen in feurigen Mitternachtsregen,
Da die Knechte mit Nesseln die sanften Augen schlugen,
Die kindlichen Früchte des Hollunders
Sich staunend neigen über ein leeres Grab.

Leise rollen vergilbte Monde
Über die Fieberlinnen des Jünglings,
Eh dem Schweigen des Winters folgt.

Ein erhabenes Schicksal sinnt den Kidron hinab,
Wo die Zeder, ein weiches Geschöpf,
Sich unter den blauen Brauen des Vaters entfaltet,
Über die Weide nachts ein Schäfer seine Herde führt.
Oder es sind Schreie im Schlaf,
Wenn ein eherner Engel im Hain den Menschen antritt,
Das Fleisch des Heiligen auf glühendem Rost hinschmilzt.

Um die Lehmhütten rankt purpurner Wein,
Tönende Bündel vergilbten Korns,
Das Summen der Bienen, der Flug des Kranichs.
Am Abend begegnen sich Auferstandene auf Felsenpfaden.

In schwarzen Wassern spiegeln sich Aussätzige;
Oder sie öffnen die kotbefleckten Gewänder
Weinend dem balsamischen Wind, der vom rosigen Hügel
    weht.

Schlanke Mägde tasten durch die Gassen der Nacht,
Ob sie den liebenden Hirten fänden.
Sonnabends tönt in den Hütten sanfter Gesang.

Lasset das Lied auch des Knaben gedenken,
Seines Wahnsinns, und weißer Brauen und seines Hingangs,
Des Verwesten, der bläulich die Augen aufschlägt.
O wie traurig ist dieses Wiedersehn.

O you psalms in fiery midnight rains,
When the servants beat the gentle eyes with nettles,
The childlike fruits of the elder tree
Bend in wonder over an empty grave.

Softly yellowed moons spin
Over the young man's fever-linens,
Before the silence of winter follows.

A noble fate ponders down the valley of Kidron,
Where the cedar, a delicate creature,
Unfolds beneath the father's blue eyebrows,
At night a shepherd leads his flock across the meadow.
Or there are screams in sleep,
When an iron-willed angel approaches man in the grove,
The saint's flesh melts away on a glowing grate.

Crimson vines climb around clay cottages,
Beating sheaves of yellowed wheat,
The humming of bees, the flight of the crane.
In the evening the resurrected meet on rocky paths.

Lepers are reflected in black waters;
Or weeping they open their filth-spattered robes
To the balm scent wind blowing from the rosy hill.

Lithe maidens grope through the backstreets of night,
That they may find the amorous shepherd.
Saturdays the cottages are filled with tender singing.

Let the song also remember the boy,
His madness, and white brows and his demise,
The decayed, who, turned blue, opens his eyes.
O how sad is this reunion.

Die Stufen des Wahnsinns in schwarzen Zimmern,
Die Schatten der Alten unter der offenen Tür,
Da Helians Seele sich im rosigen Spiegel beschaut
Und Schnee und Aussatz von seiner Stirne sinken.

An den Wänden sind die Sterne erloschen
Und die weißen Gestalten des Lichts.

Dem Teppich entsteigt Gebein der Gräber,
Das Schweigen verfallener Kreuze am Hügel,
Des Weihrauchs Süße im purpurnen Nachtwind.

O ihr zerbrochenen Augen in schwarzen Mündern,
Da der Enkel in sanfter Umnachtung
Einsam dem dunkleren Ende nachsinnt,
Der stille Gott die blauen Lider über ihn senkt.

The steps of madness in black rooms,
The shadows of the old under the open door,
Where Helian's soul sees itself in a rosy mirror
And snow and leprosy drop from his forehead.

On the walls the stars have died
And the white figures of light.

Bones of graves rise from the carpet,
The silence of rotten crosses on the hill,
The sweetness of incense on the crimson night wind.

O you broken eyes in black mouths,
While the grandson peacefully mad
Ponders the darker end alone,
The silent God lowers blue eyelids upon him.

KINDHEIT

Voll Früchten der Hollunder; ruhig wohnte die Kindheit
In blauer Höhle. Über vergangenen Pfad,
Wo nun bräunlich das wilde Gras saust,
Sinnt das stille Geäst; das Rauschen des Laubs

Ein gleiches, wenn das blaue Wasser im Felsen tönt.
Sanft ist der Amsel Klage. Ein Hirt
Folgt sprachlos der Sonne, die vom herbstlichen Hügel rollt.

Ein blauer Augenblick ist nur mehr Seele.
Am Waldsaum zeigt sich ein scheues Wild und friedlich
Ruhn im Grund die alten Glocken und finsteren Weiler.

Frömmer kennst du den Sinn der dunklen Jahre,
Kühle und Herbst in einsamen Zimmern;
Und in heiliger Bläue läuten leuchtende Schritte fort.

Leise klirrt ein offenes Fenster; zu Tränen
Rührt der Anblick des verfallenen Friedhofs am Hügel,
Erinnerung an erzählte Legenden; doch manchmal erhellt sich
    die Seele,
Wenn sie frohe Menschen denkt, dunkelgoldene Frühlingstage.

CHILDHOOD

The elder bush heavy with fruit; calmly childhood dwelled
In a blue cave. Above the vanished path,
Where the wild grass hisses brownish now,
Silent branches ponder; the murmur of leaves

As when blue water roars in the rocks.
Gentle is the blackbird's lament. A shepherd
Mutely follows the sun that rolls from the autumn hill.

A blue moment is only more soul.
A shy beast emerges from the edge of the forest and
In the valley the ancient bells and gloomy hamlets rest
    peacefully.

More piously you know the meaning of dark years,
Coolness and autumn in lonely rooms;
And in holy blue luminous steps ring forth.

Softly an open window rattles; tears well up
At the sight of the ruined graveyard on the hill,
The memory of legends told; yet sometimes the soul brightens,
When it recalls happy people, dark-gold days of spring.

STUNDENLIED

Mit dunklen Blicken sehen sich die Liebenden an,
Die Blonden, Strahlenden. In starrender Finsternis
Umschlingen schmächtig sich die sehnenden Arme.

Purpurn zerbrach der Gesegneten Mund. Die runden Augen
Spiegeln das dunkle Gold des Frühlingsnachmittags,
Saum und Schwärze des Walds, Abendängste im Grün;
Vielleicht unsäglichen Vogelflug, des Ungeborenen
Pfad an finsteren Dörfern, einsamen Sommern hin
Und aus verfallener Bläue tritt bisweilen ein Abgelebtes.

Leise rauscht im Acker das gelbe Korn.
Hart ist das Leben und stählern schwingt die Sense der
    Landmann,
Fügt gewaltige Balken der Zimmermann.

Purpurn färbt sich das Laub im Herbst; der mönchische Geist
Durchwandelt heitere Tage; reif ist die Traube
Und festlich die Luft in geräumigen Höfen.
Süßer duften vergilbte Früchte; leise ist das Lachen
Des Frohen, Musik und Tanz in schattigen Kellern;
Im dämmernden Garten Schritt und Stille des verstorbenen
    Knaben.

SONG OF HOURS

With dark looks the lovers gaze at each other,
The blond, radiant ones. In rigid darkness
Their longing arms delicately entwine.

The mouths of the blessed broke crimson. The round eyes
Mirror the dark gold of the spring afternoon,
Border and blackness of the forest, twilight fears in the green;
Perhaps the ineffable flight of birds, the unborn's
Path past sinister hamlets, to lonely summers
And at times something deceased steps from decrepit blueness.

Softly the yellow corn rustles in the field.
Life is hard and the peasant swings his steel scythe,
The carpenter joins mighty beams.

In autumn leaves turn crimson; the monastic specter
Strolls through bright days; the grape is ripe
And festive the air in spacious courtyards.
Yellowed fruit smells sweeter; quiet is the laughter
Of the joyful one, music and dance in shady cellars;
In the darkening garden, the step and silence of the dead boy.

UNTERWEGS

Am Abend trugen sie den Fremden in die Totenkammer;
Ein Duft von Teer; das leise Rauschen roter Platanen;
Der dunkle Flug der Dohlen; am Platz zog eine Wache auf.
Die Sonne ist in schwarze Linnen gesunken; immer wieder
    kehrt dieser vergangene Abend.
Im Nebenzimmer spielt die Schwester eine Sonate von Schubert.
Sehr leise sinkt ihr Lächeln in den verfallenen Brunnen,
Der bläulich in der Dämmerung rauscht. O, wie alt ist unser
    Geschlecht.
Jemand flüstert drunten im Garten; jemand hat diesen
    schwarzen Himmel verlassen.
Auf der Kommode duften Äpfel. Großmutter zündet goldene
    Kerzen an.

O, wie mild ist der Herbst. Leise klingen unsere Schritte im
    alten Park
Unter hohen Bäumen. O, wie ernst ist das hyazinthene Antlitz
    der Dämmerung.
Der blaue Quell zu deinen Füßen, geheimnisvoll die rote Stille
    deines Munds,
Umdüstert vom Schlummer des Laubs, dem dunklen Gold
    verfallener Sonnenblumen.
Deine Lider sind schwer von Mohn und träumen leise auf
    meiner Stirne.
Sanfte Glocken durchzittern die Brust. Eine blaue Wolke
Ist dein Antlitz auf mich gesunken in der Dämmerung.

Ein Lied zur Guitarre, das in einer fremden Schenke erklingt,
Die wilden Hollunderbüsche dort, ein lang vergangener
    Novembertag,
Vertraute Schritte auf der dämmernden Stiege, der Anblick
    gebräunter Balken,
Ein offenes Fenster, an dem ein süßes Hoffen zurückblieb –
Unsäglich ist das alles, o Gott, daß man erschüttert ins Knie
    bricht.

ON THE WAY

At nightfall they carried the stranger into the chamber of the
    dead;
Odor of tar; the quiet rustle of red plane trees;
The dark flight of jackdaws; a guard entered the square.
The sun has sunk into black linen; again and again this bygone
    evening returns.
In the next room the sister plays a sonata by Schubert.
Very softly her smile sinks into the crumbling well
That murmurs bluish in the twilight. O, how old is our family.
Someone whispers in the garden below; someone has
    abandoned this black sky.
Fragrant apples on the dresser. Grandmother lights golden
    candles.

O, how mild is autumn. In the old park our steps resound softly
Beneath tall trees. O, how severe is the hyacinthine face of
    twilight.
The blue spring at your feet, mysterious your mouth's red
    silence,
Darkened by the slumber of leaves, the dark gold of withered
    sunflowers.
Your eyelids are heavy with poppy and dream silently upon my
    brow.
Gentle bells tremble through the breast. Your face,
A blue cloud, has sunk onto me in the dusk.

A song accompanies the guitar that rings out in a strange tavern,
The wild elder bushes there, a long gone November day,
Familiar steps on the darkening stairs, the sight of browned
    rafters,
An open window, at which a sweet hope stayed behind—
All this is unspeakable, O God, we fall to our knees, shaken.

O, how dark is this night. A crimson flame

O, wie dunkel ist diese Nacht. Eine purpurne Flamme
Erlosch an meinem Mund. In der Stille
Erstirbt der bangen Seele einsames Saitenspiel.
Laß, wenn trunken von Wein das Haupt in die Gosse sinkt.

Went out by my mouth. In the silence
The fearful soul's lonely lyre-play dies.
Enough, when drunk with wine the head sinks into the gutter.

LANDSCHAFT

2. Fassung

Septemberabend; traurig tönen die dunklen Rufe der Hirten
Durch das dämmernde Dorf; Feuer sprüht in der Schmiede.
Gewaltig bäumt sich ein schwarzes Pferd; die hyazinthenen
    Locken der Magd
Haschen nach der Inbrunst seiner purpurnen Nüstern.
Leise erstarrt am Saum des Waldes der Schrei der Hirschkuh
Und die gelben Blumen des Herbstes
Neigen sich sprachlos über das blaue Antlitz des Teichs.
In roter Flamme verbrannte ein Baum; aufflattern mit dunklen
    Gesichtern die Fledermäuse.

LANDSCAPE

2ⁿᵈ Version

September evening; sadly the shepherds' dark calls echo
Through the twilight village; fire sparks in the forge.
Violently a black horse rears up; the maid's hyacinthine locks
Strain at the heat of its crimson nostrils.
Softly the doe's scream freezes at the forest edge
And the yellow flowers of autumn
Bend mutely over the pond's blue face.
A tree burned down in red flames; bats flutter up with dark faces.

EINSAMKEIT

Wie tief verlassen Haus und Garten sind!
Verschleiert stehn am Bach die Silberweiden.
Die Amseln sieht man wirr das Blau durchschneiden
Und manchmal bebt das wilde Gras im Wind.

Von Weihrauch schwebt ein Duft noch im Gemach
Und einsam schaut ein Bild dort aus der Nische,
Vorm'm Fenster flüstern die Hollunderbüsche
Und fluten wunderlich dem Lichte nach.

Im Tal schwand fern ein Klang von Hörnerrufen.
Der Epheu raschelt auf den Sandsteinstufen,
Wo eine Kröte kauert, grau und alt.

Sehr leise im Reseda Bienen summen,
Indes die roten Wälder rings verstummen
In einem Himmel wolkenlos und kalt.

LONELINESS

How deeply abandoned house and garden are!
Veiled the white willows stand by the brook.
You see the crazed blackbirds cut through the blue
And sometimes the wild grass trembles in the wind.

A scent of incense still floats in the chamber
And there lonely a painting peeks from the alcove,
Before the window elder bushes are whispering
And they surge strangely after the light.

In the valley a distant ringing of horns fades away.
The ivy rustles on the sandstone steps,
Where a toad cowers, gray and old.

Bees buzz very softly in the mignonette,
While the red forests fall silent all around
In a sky cloudless and cold.

ELIS

3. Fassung

1

Vollkommen ist die Stille dieses goldenen Tags.
Unter alten Eichen
Erscheinst du, Elis, ein Ruhender mit runden Augen.

Ihre Bläue spiegelt den Schlummer der Liebenden.
An deinem Mund
Verstummen ihre rosigen Seufzer.

Am Abend zog der Fischer die schweren Netze ein.
Ein guter Hirt
Führt seine Herde am Waldsaum hin.
O! wie gerecht sind, Elis, all deine Tage.

Leise sinkt
An kahlen Mauern des Ölbaums blaue Stille,
Erstirbt eines Greisen dunkler Gesang.

Ein goldener Kahn
Schaukelt, Elis, dein Herz am einsamen Himmel.

2

Ein sanftes Glockenspiel tönt in Elis' Brust
Am Abend,
Da sein Haupt ins schwarze Kissen sinkt.

Ein blaues Wild
Blutet leise im Dornengestrüpp.

Ein brauner Baum steht abgeschieden da;
Seine blauen Früchte fielen von ihm.

ELIS

1

Perfect is the silence of this golden day.
Beneath ancient oaks
You appear, Elis, a resting man with round eyes.

Their blueness mirrors the slumber of lovers.
At your mouth
Their rosy sighs fall silent.

In the evening the fisherman raised the heavy nets.
A good shepherd
Leads his flock along the forest edge.
O! how just, Elis, are all your days.

Softly
The olive tree's blue silence sinks along bare walls,
The dark song of an old man fades away.

A golden barge
Rocks, Elis, your heart against a lonely sky.

2

A faint glockenspiel sounds in Elis's breast
In the evening,
As his head sinks into the black pillow.

A blue deer
Quietly bleeds in the thicket of thorns.

A brown tree stands secluded;
Its blue fruit have fallen away.

Zeichen und Sterne
Versinken leise im Abendweiher.

Hinter dem Hügel ist es Winter geworden.

Blaue Tauben
Trinken nachts den eisigen Schweiß,
Der von Elis' kristallener Stirne rinnt.

Immer tönt
An schwarzen Mauern Gottes einsamer Wind.

Signs and stars
Sink softly into the evening pond.

Behind the hill winter has come.

Blue doves
At night drink the icy sweat
That runs from Elis's crystal brow.

Always
God's lonely wind sounds against black walls.

HOHENBURG

2. Fassung

Es ist niemand im Haus. Herbst in Zimmern;
Mondeshelle Sonate
Und das Erwachen am Saum des dämmernden Walds.

Immer denkst du das weiße Antlitz des Menschen
Ferne dem Getümmel der Zeit;
Über ein Träumendes neigt sich gerne grünes Gezweig,

Kreuz und Abend;
Umfängt den Tönenden mit purpurnen Armen sein Stern,
Der zu unbewohnten Fenstern hinaufsteigt.

Also zittert im Dunkel der Fremdling,
Da er leise die Lider über ein Menschliches aufhebt,
Das ferne ist; die Silberstimme des Windes im Hausflur.

HOHENBURG

2nd Version

No one is in the house. Autumn in rooms;
Moon-bright sonata
And the awakening at the edge of the twilight forest.

You always think the white face of mankind
Far from the turmoil of time;
Green branches bend willingly over something dreaming,

Cross and evening;
The sounding one is enfolded by the crimson arms of his star,
Which climbs to uninhabited windows.

So too the stranger trembles in the dark,
For he softly raises his eyelids over something human,
Which is far away; the silver voice of the wind in the hallway.

SEBASTIAN IM TRAUM

Für Adolf Loos

Mutter trug das Kindlein im weißen Mond,
Im Schatten des Nußbaums, uralten Hollunders,
Trunken vom Safte des Mohns, der Klage der Drossel;
Und stille
Neigte in Mitleid sich über jene ein bärtiges Antlitz

Leise im Dunkel des Fensters; und altes Hausgerät
Der Väter
Lag im Verfall; Liebe und herbstliche Träumerei.

Also dunkel der Tag des Jahrs, traurige Kindheit,
Da der Knabe leise zu kühlen Wassern, silbernen Fischen
    hinabstieg,
Ruh und Antlitz;
Da er steinern sich vor rasende Rappen warf,
In grauer Nacht sein Stern über ihn kam;

Oder wenn er an der frierenden Hand der Mutter
Abends über Sankt Peters herbstlichen Friedhof ging,
Ein zarter Leichnam stille im Dunkel der Kammer lag
Und jener die kalten Lider über ihn aufhob.

Er aber war ein kleiner Vogel im kahlen Geäst,
Die Glocke lang im Abendnovember,
Des Vaters Stille, da er im Schlaf die dämmernde
    Wendeltreppe hinabstieg.

2

Frieden der Seele. Einsamer Winterabend,
Die dunklen Gestalten der Hirten am alten Weiher;
Kindlein in der Hütte von Stroh; o wie leise
Sank in schwarzem Fieber das Antlitz hin.
Heilige Nacht.

SEBASTIAN IN A DREAM

For Adolf Loos

Mother carried the small child under the white moon,
In the shadow of the walnut tree, the ancient elder,
Drunk with the juice of poppies, the lament of the thrush;
And softly
A bearded face full of pity turned away quietly

In the window's darkness; the ancestors'
Utensils lay
Decayed; love and autumnal reverie.

Equally dark the day of year, woeful childhood,
When the boy softly descended to cool waters, silver fishes,
The silence and the face;
When he threw himself like a stone before raging black horses,
His star appeared above him in gray night;

Or when in the evenings he crossed Saint Peter's
Autumnal graveyard, holding his mother's frigid hand,
A delicate corpse lay silent in the dark chamber
And raised its cold eyelids over him.

But he was a small bird on bare branches,
The bell's long rings in November's night,
Father's silence, when sleeping he descended the twilight spiral
    stair.

2

The soul's peace. Lonely winter's eve,
The shepherds' dark shapes by the old pond;
The small child in the straw hut; o how softly
The dark face faded into black fever.
Holy night.

Oder wenn er an der harten Hand des Vaters
Stille den finstern Kalvarienberg hinanstieg
Und die dämmernden Felsennischen
Die blaue Gestalt des Menschen durch seine Legende ging,
Aus der Wunde unter dem Herzen purpurn das Blut rann.
O wie leise stand in dunkler Seele das Kreuz auf.

Liebe; da in schwarzen Winkeln der Schnee schmolz,
Ein blaues Lüftchen sich heiter im alten Hollunder fing,
In dem Schattengewölbe des Nußbaums;
Und dem Knaben leise sein rosiger Engel erschien.

Freude; da in kühlen Zimmern eine Abendsonate erklang,
Im braunen Holzgebälk
Ein blauer Falter aus der silbernen Puppe kroch.

O die Nähe des Todes. In steinerner Mauer
Neigte sich ein gelbes Haupt, schweigend das Kind,
Da in jenem März der Mond verfiel.

3

Rosige Osterglocke im Grabgewölbe der Nacht
Und die Silberstimmen der Sterne,
Daß in Schauern ein dunkler Wahnsinn von der Stirne des
    Schläfers sank.

O wie stille ein Gang den blauen Fluß hinab
Vergessenes sinnend, da im grünen Geäst
Die Drossel ein Fremdes in den Untergang rief.

Oder wenn er an der knöchernen Hand des Greisen
Abends vor die verfallene Mauer der Stadt ging
Und jener in schwarzem Mantel ein rosiges Kindlein trug,
In Schatten des Nußbaums der Geist des Bösen erschien.

Tasten über die grünen Stufen des Sommers. O wie leise
Verfiel der Garten in der braunen Stille des Herbstes,

Or when, holding his father's calloused hand,
He silently walked up Mount Calvary
And in the twilight rock niches
The blue shape of man walked through his legend,
And crimson blood flowed from the wound beneath his heart.
O how softly the cross rose in the dark soul.

Love; when in black corners the snow melted,
A blue breeze got caught brightly in the ancient elder tree,
In the shadowy vault of the walnut tree;
And the boy's rosy angel appeared softly before him.

Joy; when in cool rooms an evening sonata resounded,
In the brown woodwork
A blue moth crawled from its silvery cocoon.

O the nearness of death. In a stony wall
A yellow head turned away, the child, silent,
When that March the moon crumbled.

3

Rosy daffodils in the sepulchral vault of night
And the silver voices of stars,
So that a dark madness shivers from the sleeper's brow.

O how silent a walking down the blue river,
Pondering the forgotten, when in the green branches
The thrush called something strange to its doom.

Or when, in the evenings, holding the old man's
Bony hand, he walked to the crumbling city wall,
And carried a small rosy child in his black coat,
The spirit of evil appeared in the shade of the walnut tree.

Groping over summer's green steps. O how softly
The garden withered in autumn's brown silence,

Duft und Schwermut des alten Hollunders,
Da in Sebastians Schatten die Silberstimme des Engels erstarb.

The fragrance and sadness of the ancient elder tree,
When the angel's silvery voice died in Sebastian's shadow.

AM MOOR

3. Fassung

Wanderer im schwarzen Wind; leise flüstert das dürre Rohr
In der Stille des Moors. Am grauen Himmel
Ein Zug von wilden Vögeln folgt;
Quere über finsteren Wassern.

Aufruhr. In verfallener Hütte
Aufflattert mit schwarzen Flügeln die Fäulnis;
Verkrüppelte Birken seufzen im Wind.

Abend in verlassener Schenke. Den Heimweg umwittert
Die Sanfte Schwermut grasender Herden,
Erscheinung der Nacht: Kröten tauchen aus silbernen
    Wassern.

BY THE MOOR

3rd Version

Wayfarer in the black wind; dry reeds whisper softly
In the silence of the moor. Against the gray sky
Lines of wild birds follow;
Crossings over dark waters.

Uproar. In a dilapidated shack
Decay's black wings flutter up;
Crippled birches moan in the wind.

Evening in a deserted tavern. The way home is
Fraught with the gentle gloom of grazing herds,
Night's apparitions: toads emerge from silvery waters.

IM FRÜHLING

Leise sank von dunklen Schritten der Schnee,
Im Schatten des Baums
Heben die rosigen Lider Liebende.

Immer folgt den dunklen Rufen der Schiffer
Stern und Nacht;
Und die Ruder schlagen leise im Takt.

Balde an verfallener Mauer blühen
Die Veilchen,
Ergrünt so stille die Schläfe des Einsamen.

IN SPRING

The snow sank softly beneath dark steps,
In the shadow of the tree
Lovers raise their rosy eyelids.

Star and night forever follow
The skipper's ominous calls;
And the oars silently row as one.

Soon violets will bloom
By crumbling walls,
And so the lonely one's brow quietly greens again.

ABEND IN LANS

2. Fassung

Wanderschaft durch dämmernden Sommer
An Bündeln vergilbten Korns vorbei. Unter getünchten Bogen,
Wo die Schwalbe aus und ein flog, tranken wir feurigen Wein.

Schön: o Schwermut und purpurnes Lachen.
Abend und die dunklen Düfte des Grüns
Kühlen mit Schauern die glühende Stirne uns.

Silberne Wasser rinnen über die Stufen des Walds,
Die Nacht und sprachlos ein vergessenes Leben.
Freund; die belaubten Stege ins Dorf.

EVENING IN LANS

2nd Version

On foot through the twilight of summer,
Past sheaves of yellowed wheat. Under whitewashed arches,
Where the swallow flew in and out, we drank fiery wine.

Beautiful: o sadness and crimson laughter.
Evening and the somber scents of green
Cool our burning brows with shivers.

Silvery waters trickle down the forest steps,
Night and speechless a forgotten life.
Friend; the leaved footpaths to the village.

AM MÖNCHSBERG

2. Fassung

Wo im Schatten herbstlicher Ulmen der verfallene Pfad
   hinabsinkt,
Ferne den Hütten von Laub, schlafenden Hirten,
Immer folgt dem Wandrer die dunkle Gestalt der Kühle

Über knöchernen Steg, die hyazinthene Stimme des Knaben,
Leise sagend die vergessene Legende des Walds,
Sanfter ein Krankes nun die wilde Klage des Bruders.

Also rührt ein spärliches Grün das Knie des Fremdlings,
Das versteinerte Haupt;
Näher rauscht der blaue Quell die Klage der Frauen.

BY THE MÖNCHSBERG

2ⁿᵈ Version

Where in the shade of autumn elms the crumbling path falls
    away,
Far from leaved cottages, sleeping shepherds,
Always chill's dark figure follows the wayfarer

Over the path of bones, the boy's hyacinth voice
Quietly speaks the forest's lost legend,
Softer something dying now the brother's lament,

Thus a sparse green moves the stranger's knee,
The petrified head;
Closer the blue wellspring soughs the women's plaint.

KASPAR HAUSER LIED

Für Bessie Loos

Er wahrlich liebte die Sonne, die purpurn den Hügel
    hinabstieg,
Die Wege des Walds, den singenden Schwarzvogel
Und die Freude des Grüns.

Ernsthaft war sein Wohnen im Schatten des Baums
Und rein sein Antlitz.
Gott sprach eine sanfte Flamme zu seinem Herzen:
O Mensch!

Stille fand sein Schritt die Stadt am Abend;
Die dunkle Klage seines Munds:
Ich will ein Reiter werden.

Ihm aber folgte Busch und Tier,
Haus und Dämmergarten weißer Menschen
Und sein Mörder suchte nach ihm.

Frühling und Sommer und schön der Herbst
Des Gerechten, sein leiser Schritt
An den dunklen Zimmern Träumender hin.
Nachts blieb er mit seinem Stern allein;

Sah, daß Schnee fiel in kahles Gezweig
Und im dämmernden Hausflur den Schatten des Mörders.

Silbern sank des Ungebornen Haupt hin.

KASPAR HAUSER SONG

For Bessie Loos

He truly loved the sun climbing crimson down the hill,
The forest paths, the singing blackbird
And the delight of green.

Earnest was his life in the shade of the tree
And pure his face.
God spoke a gentle flame to his heart:
O human!

Silent his step found the city by evening;
His mouth's dark lament:
I want to be a horseman.

But shrub and beast followed him,
House and twilight garden of white people
And his murderer searched for him.

Spring and summer and the righteous one's
Lovely autumn, his quiet steps
Past the dreamers' dark rooms.
At night he remained alone with his star;

Saw that snow fell onto leafless branches
And the murderer's shadow in the twilight corridor.

Silvery the head of the unborn sank away.

NACHTS

Die Bläue meiner Augen ist erloschen in dieser Nacht,
Das rote Gold meines Herzens. O! wie stille brannte das Licht.
Dein blauer Mantel umfing den Sinkenden;
Dein roter Mund besiegelte des Freundes Umnachtung.

AT NIGHT

The blueness of my eyes has faded in this night,
The red gold of my heart. O! how softly the light burned.
Your blue coat enfolded the one drowning;
Your red mouth sealed the friend's aberration.

IM PARK

Wieder wandelnd im alten Park,
O! Stille gelb und roter Blumen.
Ihr auch trauert, ihr sanften Götter,
Und das herbstliche Gold der Ulme.
Reglos ragt am bläulichen Weiher
Das Rohr, verstummt am Abend die Drossel.
O! dann neige auch du die Stirne
Vor der Ahnen verfallenem Marmor.

IN THE PARK

Strolling again in the old park,
O! silence of yellow and red flowers.
You also mourn, you gentle gods,
And the autumn gold of the elm tree.
Motionless the reeds loom by the bluish
Pond, the thrush falls silent at night.
O! then you too shall bow your head
Before the decayed ancestral marble.

EIN WINTERABEND

2. Fassung

Wenn der Schnee ans Fenster fällt,
Lang die Abendglocke läutet,
Vielen ist der Tisch bereitet
Und das Haus ist wohlbestellt.

Mancher auf der Wanderschaft
Kommt ans Tor auf dunklen Pfaden.
Golden blüht der Baum der Gnaden
Aus der Erde kühlem Saft.

Wanderer tritt still herein;
Schmerz versteinerte die Schwelle.
Da erglänzt in reiner Helle
Auf dem Tisch Brot und Wein.

A WINTER EVENING

2nd Version

When the snow falls against the window,
The evening bell chimes long,
The table is set for many guests
And the house is well in order.

Many a traveler arrives
At the gate by dark paths.
Golden blooms the tree of mercies
From the earth's cool sap.

The traveler enters in silence;
Pain petrifies the threshold.
Then on the table bread and wine
Begin to shine in pure brightness.

DIE VERFLUCHTEN

1

Es dämmert. Zum Brunnen gehn die alten Fraun.
Im Dunkel der Kastanien lacht ein Rot.
Aus einem Laden rinnt ein Duft von Brot
Und Sonnenblumen sinken übern Zaun.

Am Fluß die Schenke tönt noch lau und leis.
Guitarre summt; ein Klimperklang von Geld.
Ein Heiligenschein auf jene Kleine fällt,
Die vor der Glastür wartet sanft und weiß.

O! blauer Glanz, den sie in Scheiben weckt,
Umrahmt von Dornen, schwarz und starrverzückt.
Ein krummer Schreiber lächelt wie verrückt
Ins Wasser, das ein wilder Aufruhr schreckt.

2

Am Abend säumt die Pest ihr blau Gewand
Und leise schließt die Tür ein finstrer Gast.
Durchs Fenster sinkt des Ahorns schwarze Last;
Ein Knabe legt die Stirn in ihre Hand.

Oft sinken ihre Lider bös und schwer.
Des Kindes Hände rinnen durch ihr Haar
Und seine Tränen stürzen heiß und klar
In ihre Augenhöhlen schwarz und leer.

Ein Nest von scharlachfarbnen Schlangen bäumt
Sich träg in ihrem aufgewühlten Schoß.
Die Arme lassen ein Erstorbenes los,
Das eines Teppichs Traurigkeit umsäumt.

THE DAMNED

1

Dusk is falling. The old women go to the well.
In the darkness of the chestnuts a red laughs.
A scent of bread escapes from a shop
And sunflowers sink over the fence.

By the river the tavern still sounds mild and low.
A guitar hums; a jangling of coins.
A halo falls upon the girl who waits
Before the glass door, soft and white.

O! blue luster she wakens in the panes,
Framed by thorns, black and stiffly rapt.
A stooping scribe smiles as if mad
Into water startled by a wild rebellion.

2

In the evening the plague hems her blue gown
And a sinister guest gently closes the door.
The maple's black burden sinks through the window;
A boy lays his brow in her hand.

Often her eyelids lower heavy and wicked.
The child's hands flow through her hair
And his tears fall hot and clear
Into the black and empty sockets of her eyes.

A nest of scarlet snakes rises
Languidly in her ruffled womb.
The arms release a thing deceased,
Hemmed in by the sadness of a carpet.

3

Ins braune Gärtchen tönt ein Glockenspiel.
Im Dunkel der Kastanien schwebt ein Blau,
Der süße Mantel einer fremden Frau.
Resedenduft; und glühendes Gefühl

Des Bösen. Die feuchte Stirn beugt kalt und bleich
Sich über Unrat, drin die Ratte wühlt,
Vom Scharlachglanz der Sterne lau umspült;
Im Garten fallen Äpfel dumpf und weich.

Die Nacht ist schwarz. Gespenstisch bläht der Föhn
Des wandelnden Knaben weißes Schlafgewand
Und leise greift in seinen Mund die Hand
Der Toten. Sonja lächelt sanft und schön.

3

A carillon sounds into the small brown garden.
In the darkness of the chestnuts a blue floats,
The sweet coat of an unknown woman.
Fragrance of mignonettes; a fiery sense

Of evil. Cold and pale the damp brow bends
Over the filth where the rat roots,
Bathed mildly by the scarlet luster of stars;
In the garden apples fall dull and soft.

The night is black. Ghostlike the föhn swells
The wandering boy's white nightgown
And quietly the hand of the dead woman seizes
His mouth. Sonja smiles soft and fair.

SONJA

Abend kehrt in alten Garten;
Sonjas Leben, blaue Stille.
Wilder Vögel Wanderfahrten;
Kahler Baum in Herbst und Stille.

Sonnenblume, sanftgeneigte
Über Sonjas weißes Leben.
Wunde, rote, niegezeigte
Läßt in dunklen Zimmern leben,

Wo die blauen Glocken läuten;
Sonjas Schritt und sanfte Stille.
Sterbend Tier grüßt im Entgleiten,
Kahler Baum in Herbst und Stille.

Sonne alter Tage leuchtet
Über Sonjas weiße Brauen,
Schnee, der ihre Wangen feuchtet,
Und die Wildnis ihrer Brauen.

SONJA

Evening returns to the old garden;
Sonja's life, blue silence.
Wild birds' migrations;
Bare tree in autumn and silence.

Sunflower, softly bent
Over Sonja's white life.
Wound, red, never shown
In dark rooms enables life,

Where the blue bells ring;
Sonja's step and gentle silence.
A dying beast greets in parting,
Bare tree in autumn and silence.

The sun of ancient days shines
Over Sonja's white eyebrows,
Snow that moistens her cheeks,
And the wilderness of her eyebrows.

ENTLANG

Geschnitten sind Korn und Traube,
Der Weiler in Herbst und Ruh.
Hammer und Amboß klingt immerzu,
Lachen in purpurner Laube.

Astern von dunklen Zäunen
Bring dem weißen Kind.
Sag wie lang wir gestorben sind;
Sonne will schwarz erscheinen.

Rotes Fischlein im Weiher;
Stirn, die sich fürchtig belauscht;
Abendwind leise ans Fenster rauscht,
Blaues Orgelgeleier.

Stern und heimlich Gefunkel
Läßt noch einmal aufschaun.
Erscheinung der Mutter in Schmerz und Graun;
Schwarze Reseden im Dunkel.

ALONG

Cut are wheat and grapes,
The hamlet in autumn and peace.
Hammer and anvil clang without pause,
Laughter in a crimson bower.

Bring asters from dark fences
For the white child.
Say how long ago since we died;
The sun wants to rise black.

A small red fish in the pond;
Forehead that spies on itself in fear;
Evening wind softly soughs at the window,
Blue drone of organs.

Star and furtive sparkling
Allow one last glance up.
Mother appears in pain and dread;
Black mignonettes in the dark.

AFRA

Ein Kind mit braunem Haar. Gebet und Amen
Verdunkeln still die abendliche Kühle
Und Afras Lächeln rot in gelbem Rahmen
Von Sonnenblumen, Angst und grauer Schwüle.

Gehüllt in blauen Mantel sah vor Zeiten
Der Mönch sie fromm gemalt an Kirchenfenstern;
Das will in Schmerzen freundlich noch geleiten,
Wenn ihre Sterne durch sein Blut gespenstern.

Herbstuntergang; und des Hollunders Schweigen.
Die Stirne rührt des Wassers blaue Regung,
Ein härnes Tuch gelegt auf eine Bahre.

Verfaulte Früchte fallen von den Zweigen;
Unsäglich ist der Vögel Flug, Begegnung
Mit Sterbenden; dem folgen dunkle Jahre.

AFRA

2nd Version

A child with brown hair. Prayer and amen
Softly darken the evening chill
And Afra's smile red in a yellow frame
Of sunflowers, fear and gray humidity.

Long ago, the monk wrapped in a blue coat
Saw her piously painted on church windows;
In pain it shall still offer friendly guidance,
When his blood is haunted by her stars.

Autumn's sinking; and the silence of the elder.
The brow stirs the water's blue motion,
A cloth of hair laid on a bier.

Rotten fruit falls from the branches;
Ineffable is the flight of birds, encounter
With the dying; followed by dark years.

DER HERBST DES EINSAMEN

Der dunkle Herbst kehrt ein voll Frucht und Fülle,
Vergilbter Glanz von schönen Sommertagen.
Ein reines Blau tritt aus verfallener Hülle;
Der Flug der Vögel tönt von alten Sagen.
Gekeltert ist der Wein, die milde Stille
Erfüllt von leiser Antwort dunkler Fragen.

Und hier und dort ein Kreuz auf ödem Hügel;
Im roten Wald verliert sich eine Herde.
Die Wolke wandert übern Weiherspiegel;
Es ruht des Landmanns ruhige Geberde.
Sehr leise rührt des Abends blauer Flügel
Ein Dach von dürrem Stroh, die schwarze Erde.

Bald nisten Sterne in des Müden Brauen;
In kühle Stuben kehrt ein still Bescheiden
Und Engel treten leise aus den blauen
Augen der Liebenden, die sanfter leiden.
Es rauscht das Rohr; anfällt ein knöchern Grauen,
Wenn schwarz der Tau tropft von den kahlen Weiden.

AUTUMN OF THE LONELY ONE

Dark autumn arrives full of fruit and plenty,
The faded luster of lovely summer days.
A pure blue flows from its decayed shroud;
The flight of birds resounds with ancient myths.
The wine has been pressed, the mild silence
Filled with quiet replies to dark questions.

And here and there a cross on a barren hill;
A herd loses itself in the red forest.
The cloud travels over the pond's mirror;
The peasant's calm gestures rest quietly.
Very softly evening's blue wing stirs
A roof of parched straw, the black earth.

Soon stars will nest in the tired one's eyebrows;
A calm modesty enters cool chambers
And angels step silently from the blue
Eyes of lovers, who suffer more gently.
The reeds rustle; a bony horror strikes,
When black the dew drips from bare willows.

RUH UND SCHWEIGEN

Hirten begruben die Sonne im kahlen Wald.
Ein Fischer zog
In härenem Netz den Mond aus frierendem Weiher.

In blauem Kristall
Wohnt der bleiche Mensch, die Wang' an seine Sterne gelehnt;
Oder er neigt das Haupt in purpurnem Schlaf.

Doch immer rührt der schwarze Flug der Vögel
Den Schauenden, das Heilige blauer Blumen,
Denkt die nahe Stille Vergessenes, erloschene Engel.

Wieder nachtet die Stirne in mondenem Gestein;
Ein strahlender Jüngling
Erscheint die Schwester in Herbst und schwarzer Verwesung.

REST AND SILENCE

Shepherds buried the sun in the stark forest.
A fisherman pulled
With a net of hair the moon from a freezing pond.

The pale man
Lives inside the blue crystal, his cheek leaning against his stars;
Or he lowers his head in crimson sleep.

But always the black flight of birds moves
The one gazing, the holiness of blue flowers,
The quiet nearby reflects on things forgotten, extinguished
    angels.

Again the forehead darkens in moonlit stone;
A glowing boy
The sister appears in autumn and black decay.

ANIF

Erinnerung: Möven, gleitend über den dunklen Himmel
Männlicher Schwermut.
Stille wohnst du im Schatten der herbstlichen Esche,
Versunken in des Hügels gerechtes Maß;

Immer gehst du den grünen Fluß hinab,
Wenn es Abend geworden,
Tönende Liebe; friedlich begegnet das dunkle Wild,

Ein rosiger Mensch. Trunken von bläulicher Witterung
Rührt die Stirne das sterbende Laub
Und denkt das ernste Antlitz der Mutter;
O, wie alles ins Dunkel hinsinkt;

Die gestrengen Zimmer und das alte Gerät
Der Väter.
Dieses erschüttert die Brust des Fremdlings.
O, ihr Zeichen und Sterne.

Groß ist die Schuld des Geborenen. Weh, ihr goldenen Schauer
Des Todes,
Da die Seele kühlere Blüten träumt.

Immer schreit im kahlen Gezweig der nächtliche Vogel
Über des Mondenen Schritt,
Tönt ein eisiger Wind an den Mauern des Dorfs.

ANIF

Memory: seagulls gliding across the dark sky
Of masculine dejection.
You live silently in the shadow of the autumn ash tree,
Sunken in the hill's righteous measure;

Always you go down the green river,
When evening has arrived,
Resounding love; peacefully the dark beast appears,

A rosy man. Drunk with a bluish scent
The forehead stirs the dying leaves
And thinks the mother's somber face;
O, how everything sinks into darkness;

The stern chambers and the forefathers'
Old tools.
This shocks the stranger's breast.
O, you signs and stars.

Great is the guilt of the one born. Woe, you golden shivers
Of death,
When the soul dreams cooler blossoms.

Always the night bird shrieks in bare branches
Over moonlit striding,
An icy wind sounds at the village walls.

UNTERGANG

5. Fassung

An Karl Borromaeus Heinrich

Über den weißen Weiher
Sind die wilden Vögel fortgezogen.
Am Abend weht von unseren Sternen ein eisiger Wind.

Über unsere Gräber
Beugt sich die zerbrochene Stirne der Nacht.
Unter Eichen schaukeln wir auf einem silbernen Kahn.

Immer klingen die weißen Mauern der Stadt.
Unter Dornenbogen
O mein Bruder klimmen wir blinde Zeiger gen Mitternacht.

RUIN

5th Version

To Karl Borromaeus Heinrich

Over the white pond
The wild birds have passed away.
In the evening an icy wind blows from our stars.

Over our graves
Bends night's shattered forehead.
Beneath oak trees we rock in a silver boat.

The city's white walls sound incessantly.
Beneath an arch of thorns
O my brother we climb blind clock hands toward midnight.

AN EINEN FRÜHVERSTORBENEN

O, der schwarze Engel, der leise aus dem Innern des Baums trat,
Da wir sanfte Gespielen am Abend waren,
Am Rand des bläulichen Brunnens.
Ruhig war unser Schritt, die runden Augen in der braunen
    Kühle des Herbstes,
O, die purpurne Süße der Sterne.

Jener aber ging die steinernen Stufen des Mönchsbergs hinab,
Ein blaues Lächeln im Antlitz und seltsam verpuppt
In seine stillere Kindheit und starb;
Und im Garten blieb das silberne Antlitz des Freundes zurück,
Lauschend im Laub oder im alten Gestein.

Seele sang den Tod, die grüne Verwesung des Fleisches
Und es war das Rauschen des Walds,
Die inbrünstige Klage des Wildes.
Immer klangen von dämmernden Türmen die blauen Glocken
    des Abends.

Stunde kam, da jener die Schatten in purpurner Sonne sah,
Die Schatten der Fäulnis in kahlem Geäst;
Abend, da an dämmernder Mauer die Amsel sang,
Der Geist des Frühverstorbenen stille im Zimmer erschien.

O, das Blut, das aus der Kehle des Tönenden rinnt,
Blaue Blume; o die feurige Träne
Geweint in die Nacht.

Goldene Wolke und Zeit. In einsamer Kammer
Lädst du öfter den Toten zu Gast,
Wandelst in trautem Gespräch unter Ulmen den grünen Fluß
    hinab.

TO ONE WHO DIED YOUNG

O, the black angel who emerged from the tree's core,
When in the evening we were gentle playmates,
By the edge of the bluish fountain.
Calm was our striding, the round eyes in the brown chill of
    autumn,
O, the crimson sweetness of the stars.

But he descended the stone steps of the Mönchsberg,
A blue smile on his face and strangely pupated,
Into his quieter childhood and died;
And in the garden the friend's silvery face remained,
Listening in the leaves or ancient rock.

The soul sang death, the flesh's green decay
And it was the murmur of the forest,
The fervent lament of the deer.
Always, the blue bells of evening sounded from twilight towers.

The hour came, when he saw shadows in the crimson sun,
The shadows of rot in bare branches;
Evening, when the blackbird sang near the twilight wall,
The spirit of the one who died young appeared silently in the
    room.

O, the blood that flows from the resounding throat,
Blue flower; o the fiery tear
Wept into the night.

Golden cloud and time. In a solitary chamber
You often invite the one who died,
And beneath elm trees, you walk in familiar conversation down
    the green river.

GEISTLICHE DÄMMERUNG

2. Fassung

Stille begegnet am Saum des Waldes
Ein dunkles Wild;
Am Hügel endet leise der Abendwind,

Verstummt die Klage der Amsel,
Und die sanften Flöten des Herbstes
Schweigen im Rohr.

Auf schwarzer Wolke
Befährst du trunken von Mohn
Den nächtigen Weiher,

Den Sternenhimmel.
Immer tönt der Schwester mondene Stimme
Durch die geistliche Nacht.

SPIRITUAL TWILIGHT

2nd Version

Silently a dark deer appears
At the forest edge;
By the hill the evening wind dies down softly,

The blackbird's lament falls silent,
And the gentle flutes of autumn
Are soundless in the reeds.

On a black cloud,
You, drunk on poppy,
Travel the nightly pond,

The starry sky.
Always the sister's lunar voice
Sounds through the spiritual night.

ABENDLÄNDISCHES LIED

O der Seele nächtlicher Flügelschlag:
Hirten gingen wir einst an dämmernden Wäldern hin
Und es folgte das rote Wild, die grüne Blume und der lallende
    Quell
Demutsvoll. O, der uralte Ton des Heimchens,
Blut blühend am Opferstein
Und der Schrei des einsamen Vogels über der grünen Stille des
    Teichs.

O, ihr Kreuzzüge und glühenden Martern
Des Fleisches, Fallen purpurner Früchte
Im Abendgarten, wo vor Zeiten die frommen Jünger gegangen,
Kriegsleute nun, erwachend aus Wunden und Sternenträumen.
O, das sanfte Zyanenbündel der Nacht.

O, ihr Zeiten der Stille und goldener Herbste,
Da wir friedliche Mönche die purpurne Traube gekeltert;
Und rings erglänzten Hügel und Wald.
O, ihr Jagden und Schlösser; Ruh des Abends,
Da in seiner Kammer der Mensch Gerechtes sann,
In stummem Gebet um Gottes lebendiges Haupt rang.

O, die bittere Stunde des Untergangs,
Da wir ein steinernes Antlitz in schwarzen Wassern beschaun.
Aber strahlend heben die silbernen Lider die Liebenden:
Ein Geschlecht. Weihrauch strömt von rosigen Kissen
Und der süße Gesang der Auferstandenen.

OCCIDENTAL SONG

O the soul's nightly stroke of the wing:
As shepherds we once walked along the twilight forests
And the red deer, the green flower and the babbling spring
Followed humbly. O, the house cricket's ancient call,
Blood blossoming on the altar stone
And the lonely bird's squall above the green silence of the pond.

O, you crusades and burning torments
Of the flesh, the fall of crimson fruit
In the evening garden, where pious disciples walked long ago,
Warriors now, waking from wounds and starry dreams.
O, night's gentle bundle of cyan.

O, you times of silence and golden autumns,
When peaceful monks we pressed the crimson grape;
And all around hills and forests sparkled.
O, you hunts and castles; evening peace,
When mankind in its chamber dwelled on righteous thoughts,
In mute prayers soared around God's living head.

O, the bitter hours of ruin,
When we behold a stone face in black waters.
But shining, lovers raise their silvery eyelids:
A race. Incense streams from rosy pillows
And the sweet chanting of the resurrected.

VERKLÄRUNG

Wenn es Abend wird,
Verläßt dich leise ein blaues Antlitz.
Ein kleiner Vogel singt im Tamarindenbaum.

Ein sanfter Mönch
Faltet die erstorbenen Hände.
Ein weißer Engel sucht Marien heim.

Ein nächtiger Kranz
Von Veilchen, Korn und purpurnen Trauben
Ist das Jahr des Schauenden.

Zu deinen Füßen
Öffnen sich die Gräber der Toten,
Wenn du die Stirne in die silbernen Hände legst.

Stille wohnt
An deinem Mund der herbstliche Mond,
Trunken von Mohnsaft dunkler Gesang;

Blaue Blume,
Die leise tönt in vergilbtem Gestein.

TRANSFIGURATION

When evening comes,
A blue face softly leaves you.
A small bird sings in the tamarind tree.

A gentle monk
Folds the lifeless hands.
A white angel visits the three Marys.

A nightly wreath
Of violets, wheat and crimson grapes
Is the year of the one who watches.

At your feet
The graves of the dead open,
When you lay your forehead into silver hands.

The autumn moon
Lives quietly at your mouth,
Drunk on the dark song of poppy juice;

Blue flower,
Softly sounding in yellowed stone.

FÖHN

Blinde Klage im Wind, mondende Wintertage,
Kindheit, leise verhallen die Schritte an schwarzer Hecke,
Langes Abendgeläut.
Leise kommt die weiße Nacht gezogen,

Verwandelt in purpurne Träume Schmerz und Plage
Des steinigen Lebens,
Daß nimmer der dornige Stachel ablasse vom verwesenden Leib.

Tief im Schlummer aufseufzt die bange Seele,

Tief der Wind in zerbrochenen Bäumen,
Und es schwankt die Klagegestalt
Der Mutter durch den einsamen Wald

Dieser schweigenden Trauer; Nächte,
Erfüllt von Tränen, feurigen Engeln.
Silbern zerschellt an kahler Mauer ein kindlich Gerippe.

FÖHN WIND

Blind lament in the wind, moonlike winter days,
Childhood, softly footsteps fade away by the black hedge,
Long peal of evening bells.
Quietly the white night draws near.

Transforms into crimson dreams the pain and trouble
Of the stony life,
So the thorny sting will never leave off the decaying body.

Deep in slumber the frightened soul sighs,

Deep the wind in broken trees,
And the mother's lamenting shape
Staggers through the lonely forest

Of this mute grief; nights
Filled with tears, fiery angels.
A child's skeleton shatters silver against the bare wall.

DER WANDERER

2. Fassung

Immer lehnt am Hügel die weiße Nacht,
Wo in Silbertönen die Pappel ragt,
Stern' und Steine sind.

Schlafend wölbt sich über den Gießbach der Steg,
Folgt dem Knaben ein erstorbenes Antlitz,
Sichelmond in rosiger Schlucht

Ferne preisenden Hirten. In altem Gestein
Schaut aus kristallenen Augen die Kröte,
Erwacht der blühende Wind, die Vogelstimme des
	Totengleichen
Und die Schritte ergrünen leise im Wald.

Dieses erinnert an Baum und Tier. Langsame Stufen von Moos;
Und der Mond,
Der glänzend in traurigen Wassern versinkt.

Jener kehrt wieder und wandelt an grünem Gestade,
Schaukelt auf schwarzem Gondelschiffchen durch die verfallene
	Stadt.

THE WAYFARER

2nd Version

Always the white night leans against the hill,
Where the poplar looms in silver shades,
Stars and stones are.

Sleeping the footbridge arches across the bourn,
A dead face follows the boy,
Sickle moon in a rosy gorge

Far from praising shepherds. In old rock
The toad peers from crystal eyes,
The blooming wind awakens, the bird voice of the deathlike
     man
And the footsteps grow quietly green in the forest.

This recalls tree and animal. Slow steps of moss;
And the moon
That glowing sinks into sad waters.

He returns and walks the green shore,
Rocks in a small black gondola through the crumbled city.

KARL KRAUS

Weißer Hohepriester der Wahrheit,
Kristallne Stimme, in der Gottes eisiger Odem wohnt,
Zürnender Magier,
Dem unter flammendem Mantel der blaue Panzer des Kriegers
    klirrt.

KARL KRAUS

White high priest of truth,
Crystal voice, in which God's icy breath dwells,
Raging magician,
Under whose blazing coat the warrior's blue armor rattles.

AN DIE VERSTUMMTEN

O, der Wahnsinn der großen Stadt, da am Abend
An schwarzer Mauer verkrüppelte Bäume starren,
Aus silberner Maske der Geist des Bösen schaut;
Licht mit magnetischer Geißel die steinerne Nacht verdrängt.
O, das versunkene Läuten der Abendglocken.

Hure, die in eisigen Schauern ein totes Kindlein gebärt.
Rasend peitscht Gottes Zorn die Stirne des Besessenen,
Purpurne Seuche, Hunger, der grüne Augen zerbricht.
O, das gräßliche Lachen des Golds.

Aber stille blutet in dunkler Höhle stummere Menschheit,
Fügt aus harten Metallen das erlösende Haupt.

TO THE ONES WHO FELL SILENT

O, the madness of the big city, when in the evening
Crippled trees stare by the black wall,
The spirit of evil watches from its silvery mask;
Light drives out the stony night with a magnetic whip.
O, the sunken chime of evening bells.

The whore who with icy chills gives birth to a dead child.
God's wrath furiously lashes the forehead of the one possessed,
Crimson plague, hunger that bursts green eyes.
O, gold's horrific laughter.

But a muter mankind bleeds softly in a dark cave,
Forging the redeeming head from hard metals.

PASSION

3. Fassung

Wenn Orpheus silbern die Laute rührt,
Beklagend ein Totes im Abendgarten,
Wer bist du Ruhendes unter hohen Bäumen?
Es rauscht die Klage das herbstliche Rohr,
Der blaue Teich,
Hinsterbend unter grünenden Bäumen
Und folgend dem Schatten der Schwester;
Dunkle Liebe
Eines wilden Geschlechts,
Dem auf goldenen Rädern der Tag davonrauscht.
Stille Nacht.

Unter finsteren Tannen
Mischten zwei Wölfe ihr Blut
In steinerner Umarmung; ein Goldnes
Verlor sich die Wolke über dem Steg,
Geduld und Schweigen der Kindheit.
Wieder begegnet der zarte Leichnam
Am Tritonsteich
Schlummernd in seinem hyazinthenen Haar.
Daß endlich zerbräche das kühle Haupt!

Denn immer folgt, ein blaues Wild,
Ein Äugendes unter dämmernden Bäumen,
Dieser dunkleren Pfaden
Wachend und bewegt von nächtigem Wohllaut,
Sanftem Wahnsinn;
Oder es tönte dunkler Verzückung
Voll das Saitenspiel
Zu den kühlen Füßen der Büßerin
In der steinernen Stadt.

PASSION

When Orpheus stirs the lute silvery,
Mourning something dead in the evening garden.
Who are you, calm thing beneath tall trees?
Autumnal reeds rustle their laments,
The blue pond,
Dying away beneath greening trees
And following the sister's shadow;
Dark love
Of a savage race,
Whose day rushes away on golden wheels.
Silent night.

Beneath sinister firs
Two wolves share their blood
In a stony embrace; the cloud
Lost something golden above the footbridge,
Childhood's patience and silence.
Again the delicate corpse appears
At the pond of Triton,
Slumbering in his hyacinth hair.
If only the cool head would finally shatter!

For always a blue deer,
Something keeping watch beneath twilight trees,
Follows these darker paths
Waking and moved by nightly harmonies,
Gentle madness;
Or the lute sounded
Full of dark rapture
At the cool feet of the penitent woman
In the city of stone.

SIEBENGESANG DES TODES

Bläulich dämmert der Frühling; unter saugenden Bäumen
Wandert ein Dunkles in Abend und Untergang,
Lauschend der sanften Klage der Amsel.
Schweigend erscheint die Nacht, ein blutendes Wild,
Das langsam hinsinkt am Hügel.

In feuchter Luft schwankt blühendes Apfelgezweig,
Löst silbern sich Verschlungenes,
Hinsterbend aus nächtigen Augen; fallende Sterne;
Sanfter Gesang der Kindheit.

Erscheinender stieg der Schläfer den schwarzen Wald hinab,
Und es rauschte ein blauer Quell im Grund,
Daß jener leise die bleichen Lider aufhob
Über sein schneeiges Antlitz;

Und es jagte der Mond ein rotes Tier
Aus seiner Höhle;
Und es starb in Seufzern die dunkle Klage der Frauen.

Strahlender hob die Hände zu seinem Stern
Der weiße Fremdling;
Schweigend verläßt ein Totes das verfallene Haus.

O des Menschen verweste Gestalt: gefügt aus kalten Metallen,
Nacht und Schrecken versunkener Wälder
Und der sengenden Wildnis des Tiers;
Windesstille der Seele.

Auf schwärzlichem Kahn fuhr jener schimmernde Ströme
    hinab,
Purpurner Sterne voll, und es sank
Friedlich das ergrünte Gezweig auf ihn,
Mohn aus silberner Wolke.

SEVENFOLD SONG OF DEATH

Spring dawns in shades of blue; beneath sucking trees
Something dark walks into evening and doom,
Listening to the blackbird's gentle lament.
Night appears in silence, a bleeding deer
That slowly sinks down by the hillside.

Blooming apple branches sway in moist air,
What is entwined comes silvery undone,
Dying out of nightly eyes; falling stars;
Soft singing of childhood.

Appearing, the one sleeping descended the black forest,
And a blue wellspring rushed in the ground,
So that he quietly raised pale eyelids
Over his snowy face;

And the moon chased a red animal
From its cave;
And the women's dark lament died sighing.

More radiantly the white stranger raised his hands
To his star;
Something dead mutely leaves the crumbled house.

O mankind's decayed shape: forged from cold metals,
Night and terror of sunken forests
And the animal's scorching wilderness;
Windless calm of the soul.

On a blackish barge he traveled down the iridescent streams,
Full of crimson stars, and greening branches
Sank peacefully down on him,
Poppy from a silvery cloud.

WINTERNACHT

Es ist Schnee gefallen. Nach Mitternacht verläßt du betrunken von purpurnem Wein den dunklen Bezirk der Menschen, die rote Flamme ihres Herdes. O die Finsternis!

Schwarzer Frost. Die Erde ist hart, nach Bitterem schmeckt die Luft. Deine Sterne schließen sich zu bösen Zeichen.

Mit versteinerten Schritten stampfst du am Bahndamm hin, mit runden Augen, wie ein Soldat, der eine schwarze Schanze stürmt. Avanti!
Bitterer Schnee und Mond!

Ein roter Wolf, den ein Engel würgt. Deine Beine klirren schreitend wie blaues Eis und ein Lächeln voll Trauer und Hochmut hat dein Antlitz versteinert und die Stirne erbleicht vor der Wollust des Frostes;

oder sie neigt sich schweigend über den Schlaf eines Wächters, der in seiner hölzernen Hütte hinsank.

Frost und Rauch. Ein weißes Sternenhemd verbrennt die tragenden Schultern und Gottes Geier zerfleischen dein metallenes Herz.

O der steinerne Hügel. Stille schmilzt und vergessen der kühle Leib im silbernen Schnee hin.

Schwarz ist der Schlaf. Das Ohr folgt lange den Pfaden der Sterne im Eis.

Beim Erwachen klangen die Glocken im Dorf. Aus dem östlichen Tor trat silbern der rosige Tag.

WINTER NIGHT

Snow has fallen. After midnight, drunk on crimson wine you leave the dark district of mankind, the red flame of its hearth. O the darkness!

Black frost. The ground is hard, the air tastes of something bitter. Your stars close into evil signs.

With petrified steps you tramp along the railway banks, with round eyes, like a soldier who storms a black entrenchment. Avanti!
Bitter snow and moon!

A red wolf strangled by an angel. Your legs rattle in stride like blue ice and a smile full of sorrow and pride has petrified your face and your forehead pales before the lust of frost;

or it bends in silence over the sleep of a watchman who collapsed in his wooden hut.

Frost and smoke. A white shirt of stars burns the carrying shoulders and God's vultures mangle your metallic heart.

O the stony hill. Silent and forgotten the cool body melts in silvery snow.

Sleep is black. Long the ear follows the paths of the stars in the ice.

At the awakening the bells rang in the village. Silver, the rosy day emerged from the eastern gate.

IN VENEDIG

Stille in nächtigem Zimmer.
Silbern flackert der Leuchter
Vor dem singenden Odem
Des Einsamen;
Zaubrisches Rosengewölk.

Schwärzlicher Fliegenschwarm
Verdunkelt den steinernen Raum
Und es starrt von der Qual
Des goldenen Tags das Haupt
Des Heimatlosen.

Reglos nachtet das Meer.
Stern und schwärzliche Fahrt
Entschwand am Kanal.
Kind, dein kränkliches Lächeln
Folgte mir leise im Schlaf.

IN VENICE

Silence in the nightly room.
The candelabrum flickers silvery
Before the singing breath
Of the lonely one;
Enchanting clouds of roses.

A blackish swarm of flies
Darkens the lithic space
And the head of the waif
Stiffens with the agony
Of a golden day.

Lifeless the sea darkens.
Star and blackish passage
Vanished along the canal.
Child, your sickly smile
Followed me softly in sleep.

VORHÖLLE

An herbstlichen Mauern, es suchen Schatten dort
Am Hügel das tönende Gold
Weidende Abendwolken
In der Ruh verdorrter Platanen.
Dunklere Tränen odmet diese Zeit,
Verdammnis, da des Träumers Herz
Überfließt von purpurner Abendröte,
Der Schwermut der rauchenden Stadt;
Dem Schreitenden nachweht goldene Kühle,
Dem Fremdling, vom Friedhof,
Als folgte im Schatten ein zarter Leichnam.

Leise läutet der steinerne Bau;
Der Garten der Waisen, das dunkle Spital,
Ein rotes Schiff am Kanal.
Träumend steigen und sinken im Dunkel
Verwesende Menschen
Und aus schwärzlichen Toren
Treten Engel mit kalten Stirnen hervor;
Bläue, die Todesklagen der Mütter.
Es rollt durch ihr langes Haar,
Ein feuriges Rad, der runde Tag
Der Erde Qual ohne Ende.

In kühlen Zimmern ohne Sinn
Modert Gerät, mit knöchernen Händen
Tastet im Blau nach Märchen
Unheilige Kindheit,
Benagt die fette Ratte Tür und Truh,
Ein Herz
Erstarrt in schneeiger Stille.
Nachhallen die purpurnen Flüche
Des Hungers in faulendem Dunkel,
Die schwarzen Schwerter der Lüge,
Als schlüge zusammen ein ehernes Tor.

LIMBO

By autumn walls, there shadows
On the hill seek the resounding gold,
Grazing evening clouds
In the peace of seared plane trees.
This age breathes darker tears,
Damnation, when the dreamer's heart
Overflows with evening's crimson afterglow,
Melancholy of the fuming city;
From the graveyard, a golden chill wafts
After the one striding, the stranger,
As though a tender corpse followed in the shadows.

Softly the stone building tolls;
The orphans' garden, the dark asylum,
A red ship on the canal.
Rotting human beings rise
And sink in darkness, dreaming,
And from blackish gates
Emerge angels with cold brows;
Blueness, the mothers' lament for the dead.
It rolls through her long hair,
A burning wheel, the round day
Of earth's endless agony.

In cool and useless rooms
Instruments rot, with bony hands
Unhallowed childhood
Gropes for fairy tales in the blue,
When a fat rat gnaws at door and chest,
A heart
Freezes in snowy silence.
Hunger's crimson curses
Echo in putrid darkness,
The black swords of falsehood,
As though a brazen gate were slamming shut.

DIE SONNE

Täglich kommt die gelbe Sonne über den Hügel.
Schön ist der Wald, das dunkle Tier,
Der Mensch; Jäger oder Hirt.

Rötlich steigt im grünen Weiher der Fisch.
Unter dem runden Himmel
Fährt der Fischer leise im blauen Kahn.

Langsam reift die Traube, das Korn.
Wenn sich stille der Tag neigt,
Ist ein Gutes und Böses bereitet.

Wenn es Nacht wird,
Hebt der Wanderer leise die schweren Lider;
Sonne aus finsterer Schlucht bricht.

THE SUN

Daily the yellow sun rises over the hill.
The forest is beautiful, the dark beast,
Man; hunter or shepherd.

The fish rises reddish in the green pond.
Beneath the round sky
The fisherman glides softly in his blue skiff.

Slowly the grape ripens, the wheat.
When the day bows out in silence,
Good and evil are prepared.

When night falls,
The wayfarer gently lifts his heavy eyelids;
The sun breaks from a sinister gorge.

GESANG EINER GEFANGENEN AMSEL

Für Ludwig von Ficker

Dunkler Odem im grünen Gezweig.
Blaue Blümchen umschweben das Antlitz
Des Einsamen, den goldnen Schritt
Ersterbend unter dem Ölbaum.
Aufflattert mit trunknem Flügel die Nacht.
So leise blutet Demut,
Tau, der langsam tropft vom blühenden Dorn.
Strahlender Arme Erbarmen
Umfängt ein brechendes Herz.

SONG OF A CAPTIVE BLACKBIRD

For Ludwig von Ficker

Dark breath in green branches.
Small blue flowers float around
The lonely one's face, his golden stride
Dying away beneath the olive tree.
Night flutters up on drunken wings.
So softly bleeds humility,
Dew dripping slowly from a blooming thorn.
The mercy of radiant arms
Enfolds a breaking heart.

SOMMER

Am Abend schweigt die Klage
Des Kuckucks im Wald.
Tiefer neigt sich das Korn,
Der rote Mohn.

Schwarzes Gewitter droht
Über dem Hügel.
Das alte Lied der Grille
Erstirbt im Feld.

Nimmer regt sich das Laub
Der Kastanie.
Auf der Wendeltreppe
Rauscht dein Kleid.

Stille leuchtet die Kerze
Im dunklen Zimmer;
Eine silberne Hand
Löscht sie aus;

Windstille, sternlose Nacht.

SUMMER

At evening the cuckoo's lament
Falls silent in the forest.
The wheat bows lower,
The red poppy.

A black storm threatens
Above the hill.
The cricket's ancient song
Dies down in a field.

The leaves on the chestnut
No longer stir.
Your dress rustles
On the winding stairs.

The candle shines softly
In the dark room;
A silver hand
Put it out;

Windless, starless night.

SOMMERSNEIGE

Der grüne Sommer ist so leise
Geworden, dein kristallenes Antlitz.
Am Abendweiher starben die Blumen,
Ein erschrockener Amselruf.

Vergebliche Hoffnung des Lebens. Schon rüstet
Zur Reise sich die Schwalbe im Haus
Und die Sonne versinkt am Hügel;
Schon winkt zur Sternenreise die Nacht.

Stille der Dörfer; es tönen rings
Die verlassenen Wälder. Herz,
Neige dich nun liebender
Über die ruhige Schläferin.

Der grüne Sommer ist so leise
Geworden und es läutet der Schritt
Des Fremdlings durch die silberne Nacht.
Gedächte ein blaues Wild seines Pfads,

Des Wohllauts seiner geistlichen Jahre!

THE REMAINS OF SUMMER

The green summer has become
So quiet, your crystal face.
The flowers died by the evening pond,
A blackbird's startled call.

Wasted hope of life. In the house
Already the swallow prepares for its journey
And the sun sets beyond the hill;
Already night beckons for a journey to the stars.

The silence of villages. Deserted forests
Resound in all directions. Heart,
Bend more lovingly now
Over the calm sleeping woman.

The green summer has become
So quiet, and the stranger's steps
Ring through the silver night.
If only a blue deer were to think of its path,

And the melodious sound of its spiritual years!

JAHR

Dunkle Stille der Kindheit. Unter grünenden Eschen
Weidet die Sanftmut bläulichen Blickes; goldene Ruh.
Ein Dunkles entzückt der Duft der Veilchen; schwankende Ähren
Im Abend, Samen und die goldenen Schatten der Schwermut.
Balken behaut der Zimmermann; im dämmernden Grund
Mahlt die Mühle; im Hasellaub wölbt sich ein purpurner Mund,
Männliches rot über schweigende Wasser geneigt.
Leise ist der Herbst, der Geist des Waldes; goldene Wolke
Folgt dem Einsamen, der schwarze Schatten des Enkels.
Neige in steinernem Zimmer; unter alten Zypressen
Sind der Tränen nächtige Bilder zum Quell versammelt;
Goldenes Auge des Anbeginns, dunkle Geduld des Endes.

YEAR

Dark silence of childhood. The sweet temper of a bluish
View grazes beneath greening ash trees; golden repose.
Something dark delights the scent of violets, swaying wheat
In the evening, seeds and the golden shadows of melancholy.
The carpenter squares wooden beams; the mill grinds
In the twilit vale; a crimson mouth arches in the hazel leaves,
A masculine red bending over silent waters.
Autumn is quiet, the spirit of the forest; a golden cloud
Follows the lonely one, the grandchild's black shadow.
Remains in a room of stone; beneath ancient cypress trees
The tears of nightly images gather by the well;
Golden eye of inception, dark patience of the end.

ABENDLAND

4. Fassung

Else Lasker-Schüler in Verehrung

1

Mond, als träte ein Totes
Aus blauer Höhle,
Und es fallen der Blüten
Viele über den Felsenpfad.
Silbern weint ein Krankes
Am Abendweiher,
Auf schwarzem Kahn
Hinüberstarben Liebende.

Oder es läuten die Schritte
Elis' durch den Hain
Den hyazinthenen
Wieder verhallend unter Eichen.
O des Knaben Gestalt
Geformt aus kristallenen Tränen,
Nächtigen Schatten.
Zackige Blitze erhellen die Schläfe
Die immerkühle,
Wenn am grünenden Hügel
Frühlingsgewitter ertönt.

2

So leise sind die grünen Wälder
Unsrer Heimat,
Die kristallne Woge
Hinsterbend an verfallner Mauer
Und wir haben im Schlaf geweint;
Wandern mit zögernden Schritten
An der dornigen Hecke hin
Singende im Abendsommer,

OCCIDENT

4ᵗʰ Version

In homage to Else Lasker-Schüler

1

Moon, as if a thing deceased
Emerged from a blue cave,
And an abundance of leaves
Is falling onto the stone path.
Something sick cries silvery
By the evening pond,
On a black skiff
Lovers crossed into death.

Or Elis's steps ring
Through the grove,
The hyacinth one,
Fading away again beneath oaks.
O the boy's form
Shaped by crystal tears,
Nightly shadows.
Jagged lightning lights the brow,
The ever cool one,
When a springtime storm
Resounds by the greening hill.

2

The green forests of our homeland
Are so quiet,
The crystal wave
Slowly dying by the crumbling wall
And we cried in our sleep;
Singing people walk with reluctant steps
In the evening summer,
Past the thorny hedges

In heiliger Ruh
Des fern verstrahlenden Weinbergs;
Schatten nun im kühlen Schoß
Der Nacht, trauernde Adler.
So leise schließt ein mondener Strahl
Die purpurnen Male der Schwermut.

3

Ihr großen Städte
Steinern aufgebaut
In der Ebene!
So sprachlos folgt
Der Heimatlose
Mit dunkler Stirne dem Wind,
Kahlen Bäumen am Hügel.
Ihr weithin dämmernden Ströme!
Gewaltig ängstet
Schaurige Abendröte
Im Sturmgewölk.
Ihr sterbenden Völker!
Bleiche Woge
Zerschellend am Strande der Nacht,
Fallende Sterne.

In the holy peace
Of the vineyard's distant dying light;
Shadows now in night's
Cool womb, mourning eagles.
So softly a lunar beam closes
The crimson marks of melancholy.

3

You great cities
Erected stone upon stone
On the plain!
So speechlessly
The homeless one
Follows the wind with his dark brow,
The bare trees by the hill.
You streams, dusking far into the distance!
The immense fear
Of the gruesome red sunset
In storm clouds.
You dying races!
Pale wave
Shattering on night's shore,
Falling stars.

FRÜHLING DER SEELE

Aufschrei im Schlaf; durch schwarze Gassen stürzt der Wind,
Das Blau des Frühlings winkt durch brechendes Geäst,
Purpurner Nachttau und es erlöschen rings die Sterne.
Grünlich dämmert der Fluß, silbern die alten Alleen
Und die Türme der Stadt. O sanfte Trunkenheit
Im gleitenden Kahn und die dunklen Rufe der Amsel
In kindlichen Gärten. Schon lichtet sich der rosige Flor.

Feierlich rauschen die Wasser. O die feuchten Schatten der Au,
Das schreitende Tier; Grünendes, Blütengezweig
Rührt die kristallene Stirne; schimmernder Schaukelkahn.
Leise tönt die Sonne im Rosengewölk am Hügel.
Groß ist die Stille des Tannenwalds, die ernsten Schatten am
      Fluß.

Reinheit! Reinheit! Wo sind die furchtbaren Pfade des Todes,
Des grauen steinernen Schweigens, die Felsen der Nacht
Und die friedlosen Schatten? Strahlender Sonnenabgrund.

Schwester, da ich dich fand an einsamer Lichtung
Des Waldes und Mittag war und groß das Schweigen des Tiers;
Weiße unter wilder Eiche, und es blühte silbern der Dorn.
Gewaltiges Sterben und die singende Flamme im Herzen.

Dunkler umfließen die Wasser die schönen Spiele der Fische.
Stunde der Trauer, schweigender Anblick der Sonne;
Es ist die Seele ein Fremdes auf Erden. Geistlich dämmert
Bläue über dem verhauenen Wald und es läutet
Lange eine dunkle Glocke im Dorf; friedlich Geleit.
Stille blüht die Myrthe über den weißen Lidern des Toten.

Leise tönen die Wasser im sinkenden Nachmittag
Und es grünet dunkler die Wildnis am Ufer, Freude im rosigen
      Wind;
Der sanfte Gesang des Bruders am Abendhügel.

SPRINGTIME OF THE SOUL

Sudden scream in sleep; the wind plunges through black
    alleyways,
The blue of springtime waves through snapping branches,
Crimson dew of night and all around the stars are going out.
The river dawns in greens, silver the ancient avenues
And the towers of the city. O gentle drunkenness
On the gliding boat and the blackbird's dark calls
In the childlike gardens. Already the rosy overgrowth begins to
    clear.

The waters' solemn rush. O the moist shadows of the mead,
The pacing animal; things greening, blossoming branches
Stir the crystal forehead; glimmering, rocking boat.
Gently the sun sounds in rosy clouds above the hillside.
Great is the silence of the fir forest, the grave shadows by the river.

Purity! Purity! Where are the terrible paths of death,
The gray and stony hush, the cliffs of night
And the ever-disturbed shadows? Radiant abyss of the sun.

Sister, when I found you by the lonely glade in the forest
And it was noon and the animal's silence was immense;
White girl beneath the wild oak, and the thorn bloomed silvery.
Great dying and the singing flame of the heart.

Darker the waters engulf the pretty play of fish.
Hour of grief, the sun's mute gazing;
The soul is a stranger on earth. The sacred dusking
Of blue above the mutilated forest and a dark bell
Chimes long in the village; peaceful cortège.
Silently the myrtle blooms over the dead man's white eyelids.

Quietly the waters rush in the sinking afternoon
And the wilderness by the shore greens darker, delight in rosy
    wind;
The brother's gentle song by the evening hillside.

IM DUNKEL

2. Fasung

Es schweigt die Seele den blauen Frühling.
Unter feuchtem Abendgezweig
Sank in Schauern die Stirne den Liebenden.

O das grünende Kreuz. In dunklen Gespräch
Erkannten sich Mann und Weib.
An kahler Mauer
Wandelt mit seinen Gestirnen der Einsame.

Über die mondbeglänzten Wege des Walds
Sank die Wildnis
Vergessener Jagden; Blick der Bläue
Aus verfallenen Felsen bricht.

IN DARKNESS

2ⁿᵈ Version

The soul's silence begets blue springtime.
Beneath damp evening branches
The lovers' brows sank in shivers.

O the greening cross. In somber conversations
Man and woman recognized each other.
By a bare wall
The lonely one wanders with his heavenly bodies.

The wilderness of forgotten hunts
Sank across
Moon-glazed forest paths; a blue's glance
Breaks from crumbling cliffs.

GESANG DES ABGESCHIEDENEN

An Karl Borromaeus Heinrich

Voll Harmonien ist der Flug der Vögel. Es haben die grünen
    Wälder
Am Abend sich zu stilleren Hütten versammelt;
Die kristallenen Weiden des Rehs.
Dunkles besänftigt das Plätschern des Bachs, die feuchten
    Schatten

Und die Blumen des Sommers, die schön im Winde läuten.
Schon dämmert die Stirne dem sinnenden Menschen.

Und es leuchtet ein Lämpchen, das Gute, in seinem Herzen
Und der Frieden des Mahls; denn geheiligt ist Brot und Wein
Von Gottes Händen, und es schaut aus nächtigen Augen
Stille dich der Bruder an, daß er ruhe von dorniger
    Wanderschaft.
O das Wohnen in der beseelten Bläue der Nacht.

Liebend auch umfängt das Schweigen im Zimmer die Schatten
    der Alten,
Die purpurnen Martern, Klage eines großen Geschlechts,
Das fromm nun hingeht im einsamen Enkel.

Denn strahlender immer erwacht aus schwarzen Minuten des
    Wahnsinns
Der Duldende an versteinerter Schwelle
Und es umfängt ihn gewaltig die kühle Bläue und die
    leuchtende Neige des Herbstes,

Das stille Haus und die Sagen des Waldes,
Maß und Gesetz und die mondenen Pfade der Abgeschiedenen.

SONG OF THE ONE DEPARTED

For Karl Borromaeus Heinrich

The flight of birds is full of harmonies. In the evening
The green forests have gathered by quieter shacks;
The deer's crystal meadows.
Something dark soothes the brook's purl, the damp shadows

And the flowers of summer that ring lovely in the wind.
Already the pondering man's forehead is dawning.

And a little lamp of goodness shines in his heart
And the peace of the meal; for bread and wine
Are blessed by the hands of God, and your brother looks
At you softly with nightly eyes, that he may rest from thorny
    travels.
O to dwell in the soulful blue of night.

Lovingly too the silence of the room enfolds the shadows of the old,
The crimson torments, lament of a great lineage
That now passes piously in the lonely grandchild.

For the patient one wakes ever more radiantly by petrified steps
From black minutes of madness
And the cool blue embraces him mightily and the burning
    remains of autumn,

The silent house and the legends of the forest,
Measure and law and the lunar paths of the departed.

IN HELLBRUNN

Wieder folgend der blauen Klage des Abends
Am Hügel hin, am Frühlingsweiher –
Als schwebten darüber die Schatten lange Verstorbener,
Die Schatten der Kirchenfürsten, edler Frauen –
Schon blühen ihre Blumen, die ernsten Veilchen
Im Abendgrund, rauscht des blauen Quells
Kristallne Woge. So geistlich ergrünen
Die Eichen über den vergessenen Pfaden der Toten,
Die goldene Wolke über dem Weiher.

IN HELLBRUNN

Following again the blue lament of evening
Along the hill, by the springtime pond—
As if the shadows of those long dead hovered above it,
The shadows of priestly princes, noble women—
Their flowers are already in bloom, the grave violets
In the evening vale, the blue wellspring's crystal
Billow rushes. So sacred green the oak trees
Above the forgotten paths of the dead,
The golden cloud above the pond.

DAS HERZ

Das wilde Herz ward weiß am Wald;
O dunkle Angst
Des Todes, so das Gold
In grauer Wolke starb.
Novemberabend.
Am kahlen Tor am Schlachthaus stand
Der armen Frauen Schar;
In jeden Korb
Fiel faules Fleisch und Eingeweid;
Verfluchte Kost!

Des Abends blaue Taube
Brachte nicht Versöhnung.
Dunkler Trompetenruf
Durchfuhr der Ulmen
Nasses Goldlaub,
Eine zerfetzte Fahne
Vom Blute rauchend,
Daß in wilder Schwermut
Hinlauscht ein Mann.
O! ihr ehernen Zeiten
Begraben dort im Abendrot.

Aus dunklem Hausflur trat
Die goldne Gestalt
Der Jünglingin
Umgeben von bleichen Monden,
Herbstlicher Hofstaat,
Zerknickten schwarze Tannen
Im Nachtsturm,
Die steile Festung.
O Herz
Hinüberschimmernd in schneeige Kühle.

THE HEART

The wild heart grew white by the forest;
O dark fear
Of death, that gold
Died in a gray cloud.
November evening.
By the bare gate of the slaughterhouse
Stood a crowd of poor women;
Into every basket
Fell putrid meat and guts;
Cursed fare!

Evening's blue dove
Did not deliver reconciliation.
Dark trumpet blare
Passed through the elm trees'
Wet golden leaves,
A tattered flag
Steaming with blood,
So that a man eavesdrops
In wild melancholy.
O! you brazen times
Buried there in the sunset.

From a dark corridor
The golden figure
Of the girlchild emerged,
Surrounded by pale moons,
Autumnal retinue,
Snapped black fir trees
In the night storm,
The steep citadel.
O heart
Gleaming across into snowy chill.

DER SCHLAF

2. Fassung

Verflucht ihr dunklen Gifte,
Weißer Schlaf!
Dieser höchst seltsame Garten
Dämmernder Bäume
Erfüllt von Schlangen, Nachtfaltern,
Spinnen, Fledermäusen.
Fremdling! Dein verlorner Schatten
Im Abendrot.
Ein finsterer Korsar
Im salzigen Meer der Trübsal.
Aufflattern weiße Vögel am Nachtsaum
Über stürzenden Städten
Von Stahl.

SLEEP

Curse you, dark poisons,
White sleep!
This most strange garden
Of twilight trees
Filled with snakes, moths,
Spiders, bats.
Stranger! Your lost shadow
In the afterglow.
A sinister corsair
In the salty sea of misery.
White birds flutter up at night's edge
Above falling cities
Of steel.

DAS GEWITTER

Ihr wilden Gebirge, der Adler
Erhabene Trauer.
Goldnes Gewölk
Raucht über steinerner Öde.
Geduldige Stille odmen die Föhren,
Die schwarzen Lämmer am Abgrund,
Wo plötzlich die Bläue
Seltsam verstummt,
Das sanfte Summen der Hummeln.
O grüne Blume –
O Schweigen.

Traumhaft erschüttern des Wildbachs
Dunkle Geister das Herz,
Finsternis,
Die über die Schluchten hereinbricht!
Weiße Stimmen
Irrend durch schaurige Vorhöfe,
Zerrißne Terrassen,
Der Väter gewaltiger Groll, die Klage
Der Mütter,
Des Knaben goldener Kriegsschrei
Und Ungebornes
Seufzend aus blinden Augen.

O Schmerz, du flammendes Anschaun
Der großen Seele!
Schon zuckt im schwarzen Gewühl
Der Rosse und Wagen
Ein rosenschauriger Blitz
In die tönende Fichte.
Magnetische Kühle
Umschwebt dies stolze Haupt,
Glühende Schwermut
Eines zürnenden Gottes.

THE THUNDERSTORM

You wild mountains, the eagles'
Noble sorrow.
Golden clouds
Fuming above stony wasteland.
The pine trees breathe patient stillness,
The black lambs by the abyss,
Where suddenly blueness
Falls strangely silent,
The gentle hum of bumblebees.
O green flower—
O silence.

Dreamlike the mountain torrent's dark spirits
Rattle the heart,
Darkness
That descends upon the gorges!
White voices
Straying through eerie courtyards,
Torn terraces,
The fathers' immense resentment, the lament
Of mothers,
The boy's golden war cry
And something unborn
Sighing from blind eyes.

O pain, you blazing vision
Of the great soul!
Already in the black throng
Of horses and carts
A rose-horrid lightning bolt
Strikes a ringing spruce tree.
A magnetic chill
Hovers around this proud head,
The burning melancholy
Of a raging god.

Angst, du giftige Schlange,
Schwarze, stirb im Gestein!
Da stürzen der Tränen
Wilde Ströme herab,
Sturm-Erbarmen,
Hallen in drohenden Donnern
Die schneeigen Gipfel rings.
Feuer
Läutert zerrissene Nacht.

Fear, you poisonous snake,
Black one, die in the rock!
Then the tears' wild
Torrents come crashing down,
Storm-pity,
The snowy peaks all around
Echo in threatening thunder.
Fire
Purifies the torn night.

DER ABEND

Mit toten Heldengestalten
Erfüllst du Mond
Die schweigenden Wälder,
Sichelmond –
Mit der sanften Umarmung
Der Liebenden,
Den Schatten berühmter Zeiten
Die modernden Felsen rings;
So bläulich erstrahlt es
Gegen die Stadt hin,
Wo kalt und böse
Ein verwesend Geschlecht wohnt,
Der weißen Enkel
Dunkle Zukunft bereitet.
Ihr mondverschlungnen Schatten
Aufseufzend im leeren Kristall
Des Bergsees.

EVENING

With figures of dead heroes,
Moon, you fill
The silent forests,
Sickle moon—
With the soft embrace
Of lovers,
The shadows of glorious times
The decaying cliffs everywhere;
So bluish it glows
Toward the city,
Where cold and evil
A rotting lineage lives,
Preparing an ominous future
For its white grandchildren.
You moon-devoured shadows
Sighing in the empty crystal
Of the mountain lake.

DIE NACHT

Dich sing ich wilde Zerklüftung,
Im Nachtsturm
Aufgetürmtes Gebirge;
Ihr grauen Türme
Überfließend von höllischen Fratzen,
Feurigem Getier,
Rauhen Farnen, Fichten,
Kristallnen Blumen.
Unendliche Qual,
Daß du Gott erjagtest
Sanfter Geist,
Aufseufzend im Wassersturz,
In wogenden Föhren.

Golden lodern die Feuer
Der Völker rings.
Über schwärzliche Klippen
Stürzt todestrunken
Die erglühende Windsbraut,
Die blaue Woge
Des Gletschers
Und es dröhnt
Gewaltig die Glocke im Tal:
Flammen, Flüche
Und die dunklen
Spiele der Wollust,
Stürmt den Himmel
Ein versteinertes Haupt.

NIGHT

Your wild fissures I sing,
Towering mountains
In the tempest of night;
You gray flowers
Overflowing with hellish grimaces,
Blazing beasts,
Coarse ferns, firs,
Crystal flowers.
Endless agony,
That you caught God,
Gentle spirit,
Sighing in falling waters,
In surging pine trees.

Golden flare the fires
Of the races all around.
Over blackish cliffs
The glowing whirlwind
Plunges drunken with death,
The blue swell
Of the glacier
And the bell in the valley
Drones mightily:
Flames, curses
And the dark
Games of lust,
A petrified head
Storms the sky.

DIE SCHWERMUT

Gewaltig bist du dunkler Mund
Im Innern, aus Herbstgewölk
Geformte Gestalt,
Goldner Abendstille;
Ein grünlich dämmernder Bergstrom
In zerbrochner Föhren
Schattenbezirk;
Ein Dorf,
Das fromm in braunen Bildern abstirbt.

Da springen die schwarzen Pferde
Auf nebliger Weide.
Ihr Soldaten!
Vom Hügel, wo sterbend die Sonne rollt
Stürzt das lachende Blut –
Unter Eichen
Sprachlos! O grollende Schwermut
Des Heers; ein strahlender Helm
Sank klirrend von purpurner Stirne.

Herbstesnacht so kühle kommt,
Erglänzt mit Sternen
Über zerbrochenem Männergebein
Die stille Mönchin.

MELANCHOLY

You are vast, dark mouth
Within, figure shaped
By autumn clouds,
Golden evening silence;
A greenish dusky mountain stream
In the shadowy regions
Of shattered pine trees;
A village
That dies away piously in brown images.

Then the black horses
Leap on a foggy meadow.
You soldiers!
The laughing blood plunges
From the hill where the dying sun rolls—
Beneath oak trees
Speechless! O the army's glowering
Melancholy; a radiant helmet
Sank clashing from a crimson brow.

The autumn night arrives with a chill,
Gleaming with stars
Above the broken bones of men,
The silent female monk.

DIE HEIMKEHR

2. Fassung

Die Kühle dunkler Jahre,
Schmerz und Hoffnung
Bewahrt zyklopisch Gestein,
Menschenleeres Gebirge,
Des Herbstes goldner Odem,
Abendwolke –
Reinheit!

Anschaut aus blauen Augen
Kristallne Kindheit;
Unter dunklen Fichten
Liebe, Hoffnung,
Daß von feurigen Lidern
Tau ins starre Gras tropft –
Unaufhaltsam!

O! dort der goldene Steg
Zerbrechend im Schnee
Des Abgrunds!
Blaue Kühle
Odmet das nächtige Tal,
Glaube, Hoffnung!
Gegrüßt du einsamer Friedhof!

THE RETURN

Cyclopean rocks preserve
The chill of dark years,
Pain and hope,
Deserted mountains,
Autumn's golden breath,
Evening cloud—
Purity!

Crystal childhood
Gazes from blue eyes;
Beneath dark fir trees
Love, hope,
So dew drips from fiery eyelids
Into stiff grass—
Relentless!

O! there the golden footbridge
Breaking in the snow
Of the abyss!
The nightly valley
Breathes blue chill,
Faith, hope!
Greetings, desolate graveyard!

KLAGE

Jüngling aus kristallnem Munde
Sank dein goldner Blick ins Tal;
Waldes Woge rot und fahl
In der schwarzen Abendstunde.
Abend schlägt so tiefe Wunde!

Angst! des Todes Traumbeschwerde,
Abgestorben Grab und gar
Schaut aus Baum und Wild das Jahr;
Kahles Feld und Ackererde.
Ruft der Hirt die bange Herde.

Schwester, deine blauen Brauen
Winken leise in der Nacht.
Orgel seufzt und Hölle lacht
Und es faßt das Herz ein Grauen;
Möchte Stern und Engel schauen.

Mutter muß ums Kindlein zagen;
Rot ertönt im Schacht das Erz,
Wollust, Tränen, steinern Schmerz,
Der Titanen dunkle Sagen.
Schwermut! einsam Adler klagen.

LAMENT

Youth, from your crystal mouth
Your golden gaze sank to the valley;
The forest's surge red and sallow
In the black hour of evening.
Evening strikes such a deep wound!

Fear! death's dream grievance,
Withered grave and even the year
Looks out from tree and beast;
Barren field and an acre's soil.
The shepherd calls his frightened flock.

Sister, your blue eyebrows
Softly beckon in the night.
An organ sighs and hell laughs
And terror seizes the heart;
It wants to see stars and angels.

Mother must fear for her small child;
Red the ore sounds in the shaft,
Lust, tears, stony pain,
The Titans' dark legends.
Melancholy! the eagles' lonely lament.

NACHTERGEBUNG

5. Fassung

Mönchin! schließ mich in dein Dunkel,
Ihr Gebirge kühl und blau!
Niederblutet dunkler Tau;
Kreuz ragt steil im Sterngefunkel.

Purpurn brachen Mund und Lüge
In verfallner Kammer kühl;
Scheint noch Lachen, golden Spiel,
Einer Glocke letzte Züge.

Mondeswolke! Schwärzlich fallen
Wilde Früchte nachts vom Baum
Und zum Grabe wird der Raum
Und zum Traum dies Erdenwallen.

NIGHT'S SURRENDER

5th Version

Female monk! cloister me in your darkness,
You mountains cool and blue!
Dark dew bleeds down;
A cross looms boldly amid sparkling stars.

Mouth and lie broke crimson
In the cool of a decayed chamber;
Laughter still glows, golden chime
Of a bell's final strokes.

Moon cloud! Wild fruit falls
Blackish from trees at night
And space becomes a grave
And earth's pilgrimage a dream.

IM OSTEN

Den wilden Orgeln des Wintersturms
Gleicht des Volkes finstrer Zorn,
Die purpurne Woge der Schlacht,
Entlaubter Sterne.

Mit zerbrochnen Brauen, silbernen Armen
Winkt sterbenden Soldaten die Nacht.
Im Schatten der herbstlichen Esche
Seufzen die Geister der Erschlagenen.

Dornige Wildnis umgürtet die Stadt.
Von blutenden Stufen jagt der Mond
Die erschrockenen Frauen.
Wilde Wölfe brachen durchs Tor.

IN THE EAST

The winter storm's wild organ-pipes
Resemble the dark rage of the people,
The crimson wave of battle,
Defoliated stars.

With fractured eyebrows, silver arms
Night waves to dying soldiers.
The specters of the slain
Sigh in the shade of the autumn ash.

Thorny wilderness girds the city.
The moon chases terrified women
From bleeding thresholds.
Wild wolves broke through the gate.

HÖLDERLIN

Der Wald liegt herbstlich ausgebreitet
Die Winde ruhn, ihn nicht zu wecken
Das Wild schläft friedlich in Verstecken,
Indes der Bach ganz leise gleitet.

So ward ein edles Haupt verdüstert
In seiner Schönheit Glanz und Trauer
Von Wahnsinn, den ein frommer Schauer
Am Abend durch die Kräuter flüstert.

HÖLDERLIN

The forest lies spread out in autumn
The winds rest, as not to wake it
The deer sleep peacefully in their lairs,
While a brook flows very quietly.

So a noble head was darkened
In the luster and grief of its beauty
By madness, which a pious shudder
At evening whispers through the herbs.

GRODEK

2. Fassung

Am Abend tönen die herbstlichen Wälder
Von tödlichen Waffen, die goldnen Ebenen
Und blauen Seen, darüber die Sonne
Düstrer hinrollt; umfängt die Nacht
Sterbende Krieger, die wilde Klage
Ihrer zerbrochenen Münder.
Doch stille sammelt im Weidengrund
Rotes Gewölk, darin ein zürnender Gott wohnt
Das vergoßne Blut sich, mondne Kühle;
Alle Straßen münden in schwarze Verwesung.
Unter goldnem Gezweig der Nacht und Sternen
Es schwankt der Schwester Schatten durch den schweigenden
    Hain,
Zu grüßen die Geister der Helden, die blutenden Häupter;
Und leise tönen im Rohr die dunkeln Flöten des Herbstes.
O stolzere Trauer! ihr ehernen Altäre
Die heiße Flamme des Geistes nährt heute ein gewaltiger
    Schmerz,
Die ungebornen Enkel.

GRODEK

At evening the autumnal forests resound
With deadly weapons, the golden plains
And blue lakes, above them the sun
Rolling away more sinister; night enfolds
The dying warriors, the wild lament
Of their shattered mouths.
But on the pasture spilled blood,
Red clouds in which a raging god lives,
Gathers softly, lunar chill;
All roads lead to black decay.
Beneath the golden branches of night and stars
The sister's shadow reels through the silent grove,
To greet the ghosts of heroes, the bleeding heads;
And the dark flutes of autumn sound softly in the reeds.
O prouder sorrow! you brazen altars
Today an immense pain feeds the spirit's hot flame,
The unborn descendants.

DIE DREI TEICHE IN HELLBRUNN

1. Fassung

Der erste

Um die Blumen taumelt das Fliegengeschmeiß,
Um die bleichen Blumen auf dumpfer Flut,
Geh fort! Geh fort! Es brennt die Luft!
In der Tiefe glüht der Verwesung Glut!
Die Weide weint, das Schweigen starrt,
Auf den Wassern braut ein schwüler Dunst.
Geh fort! Geh fort! Dies ist der Ort
Für schwarzer Kröten ekle Brunst.

Der zweite

Bilder von Wolken, Blumen und Menschen –
Singe, singe, freudige Welt!
Lächelnde Unschuld spiegelt dich wider –
Himmlisch wird alles, was ihr gefällt!
Dunkles wandelt sie freundlich in Helle,
Fernes wird nah! O Freudiger du!
Sonne, Wolken, Blumen und Menschen
Atmen in dir Gottesruh.

Der dritte

Die Wasser schimmern grünlich-blau
Und ruhig atmen die Zypressen,
Es tönt der Abend glockentief –
Da wächst die Tiefe unermessen.
Der Mond steigt auf, es blaut die Nacht,
Erblüht im Widerschein der Fluten –
Ein rätselvolles Sphinxgesicht,
Daran mein Herz sich will verbluten.

THE THREE PONDS IN HELLBRUNN

1st Version

The First

A rabble of flies whirls around the flowers,
Around the pale flowers on a stifling flood,
Begone! Begone! The air is burning!
Decay's embers glow in the depth!
The willow weeps, silence stares,
A sultry mist brews on the waters.
Begone! Begone! This place is for
The foul rut of black toads.

The Second

Images of clouds, flowers and people—
Sing, sing, joyful world!
Smiling innocence reflects you—
Everything that pleases it becomes divine!
Kindly it transforms darkness into light,
The distant into the near! O you joyful one!
Sun, clouds, flowers and people
God's blissful peace breathes inside you.

The Third

The waters shimmer in greens and blues
And the cypresses breathe calmly,
Evening sounds in deep bells—
When depth grows immeasurably.
The moon rises, night is turning blue,
Blossoms in the floods' reflection—
The mysterious face of the Sphinx,
On which my heart wishes to bleed out.

About the Author

GEORG TRAKL (1887 – 1914) is commonly seen as one of the leading figures of the Austro-German expressionist movement in literature during the early part of the twentieth century. The fourth of six children, Trakl was born on February 3, 1887 in Salzburg, Austria, to Tobias Trakl, a protestant hardware businessman, and Maria Halik, a Catholic housewife. Tobias Trakl's fortunate business endeavors enabled the family to reside in one of the most affluent neighborhoods of Mozart's birth city. The interior of this perfect family façade, however, exposed a father's lack of interest in family life and an un-nurturing mother who was manic-depressive and addicted to opium.

Trakl attended a Catholic elementary school and, in the fall of 1897, entered the *Salzburg Staatsgymnasium*, a humanistic high school. In 1905, after having failed twice to be promoted, he dropped out of school and began an apprenticeship at the *Weisser Engel* (White Angel) pharmacy in Salzburg. It was during this time that Trakl first experimented not only with poetic expression, but with alcohol, drugs (mostly opium and cocaine), prostitutes, and attempts at suicide. He also began an incestuous relationship with his younger sister Margarete, who, born in 1891, eventually, after having become an accomplished pianist, committed suicide in Berlin in 1917.

Trakl moved to Vienna in 1908 to further his studies of pharmacy and received his degree in 1910, only a short time after his father's death. In Vienna, he became a member of a small, bohemian literary group, whose members introduced him to the works of Baudelaire, Verlaine, Rimbaud, George, Nietzsche, Dostoevsky, and von Hofmannstahl. After a mandatory year of military service, unable to bear the civilian life, Trakl reenlisted as a pharmacist for the military hospital in Innsbruck, where he met Ludwig von Ficker, the editor and publisher of a Christian existentialist journal titled *Der Brenner*. In addition to securing funds donated by Ludwig Wittgenstein for emerging poets, von Ficker was instrumental in convincing the editors of the leading publisher of literary expressionism at the time (the Kurt Wolff-Verlag in Leipzig, Germany) to publish Trakl's first and only full-length collection of poems: *Gedichte* (*Poems*) (1913).

At the outbreak of World War I in August of 1914, Trakl's medical unit was ordered to Galicia, Poland, and entered the battle of Grodek, where Austrian and Russian soldiers faced each other. At one point, Trakl was forced to oversee and care for well over ninety severely wounded soldiers. The extreme suffering he had to witness reached a breaking point when he attempted to shoot himself. His unit members, however, prevented Trakl's suicide and committed him to a mental institution in Krakow, where he shared a cell with a soldier who was suffering from delirium tremens. There, Trakl died on November 4, 1914, from an apparent overdose of cocaine.

Trakl's poetry is marked by the perpetual use of nightmarish visions of disintegration, death, and murder, as well as of natural decay. His poems bear haunting witness to a world devoid of faith, meaning, and hope. In the majority of his poems, Trakl creates a series of unconnected metaphors, a series of images and impressions, to denote the fragmentation and meaninglessness of modern existence. Truth is what Trakl attempts to detect through his poetry—more specifically, the fact that one's unconscious horror mirrors the horror we experience in reality as we try to cope with our human condition. Nevertheless, one senses that Trakl still captures glimpses of beauty in this wasteland, a beauty he usually equates with erotic or familial relationships, a beauty that in his view can only be seen in contrast with death and horror.

About the Translator

DANIELE PANTANO is a Swiss poet, essayist, literary translator, and artist. He has published over twenty volumes of poetry, essays, and translations, and his work has been translated into a dozen languages. For more information, please visit www.pantano.ch.